W9-CXV-782

The 500 Hidden Secrets of
SAN FRANCISCO

INTRODUCTION

This book invites you to venture off the beaten track and discover hidden gems tucked within the hills of San Francisco. As you leaf through the guide and examine the categories you will discover the city's renowned restaurants, secret watering holes, curious little shops and galleries, old historic places, as well as the favorite haunts of locals themselves.

The main objective of this publication is to guide the reader to the places not typically included in tourist guides. Like a secret fairy door in Golden Gate Park or the truly steepest hills in the city. At the same time it also lists fantastic places frequented by San Francisco residents, like where to shop for local goods and antiques, or where to go for a fabulous brunch and the best craft cocktails in the city.

At 11 × 11 km, San Francisco is a rather small city, but there are a million things to see and do, and plenty to taste and savor. Locals are always welcoming and willing to provide their suggestions, and places are easily accessible.

This guide does not mention everything you can see and do in San Francisco. Rather it is intended to be intimate, personal and to offer friendly insights and starting points based on experience. The author shares her favorite places with readers, much as she would do with a friend who was visiting San Francisco.

HOW TO
USE THIS BOOK?

This guide lists 500 things you need to know about San Francisco in 100 different categories. Most of these are places to visit, with practical information to help you find your way. Others are bits of information that help you get to know the city and its habitants. The aim of this guide is to inspire, not to cover the city from A to Z.

The places listed in the guide are given an address, including the neighborhood, and a number. The neighborhood and number allow you to find the locations on the maps at the beginning of the book: first look for the map of the corresponding neighborhood, then look for the right number. A word of caution: these maps are not detailed enough to allow you to find specific locations in the city. You can obtain an excellent map from any tourist office or in most hotels. Or the addresses can be located on a smartphone.

Please also bear in mind that cities change all the time. The chef who hits a high note one day may be uninspiring on the day you happen to visit. The hotel ecstatically reviewed in this book might suddenly go downhill under a new manager. The bar considered one of the 5 best places for craft cocktails might be empty on the night you visit. This is obviously a highly personal selection. You might not always agree with it. If you want to leave a comment, recommend a bar or reveal your favorite secret place, please visit the website *www.the500hiddensecrets.com* – you'll also find free tips and the latest news about the series there – or follow *@500hiddensecrets* on Instagram or Facebook and leave a comment.

THE AUTHOR

A native to San Francisco, Leslie Santarina is a freelance photographer and editor (*www.spottedsf.com*) and her work takes her to every corner of the city – to cafes, restaurants, shops, museums, exhibits and new openings. Endlessly curious about her city and its secrets, culture and history, she takes every opportunity to make new discoveries on her visits across San Francisco's many neighborhoods. Each has its distinct treasures. With a camera at hand, you'll find her continuously exploring and capturing images of these gems in her city.

Beyond visiting the most important sights, Leslie encourages you to experience the daily life in San Francisco. Her advice? Wander around aimlessly, enjoy getting lost and finding surprises along the way. Take in the views from the hilltops. Unwind at the local coffee shops. Savor the diverse culinary options and peruse the local food markets. And most of all, chat with the locals. Each offers a unique perspective and they're happy to provide additional suggestions on things to see and do in the city.

The author wishes to thank the many people who have helped her draw up the list of 500 special places in San Francisco. Her family, friends, friends of friends, colleagues, acquaintances and even strangers have proved invaluable in providing tips, advice and sharing their own favorite spots around the city. At Luster, she thanks Dettie Luyten for championing and steering this book to completion.

SAN FRANCISCO AREA

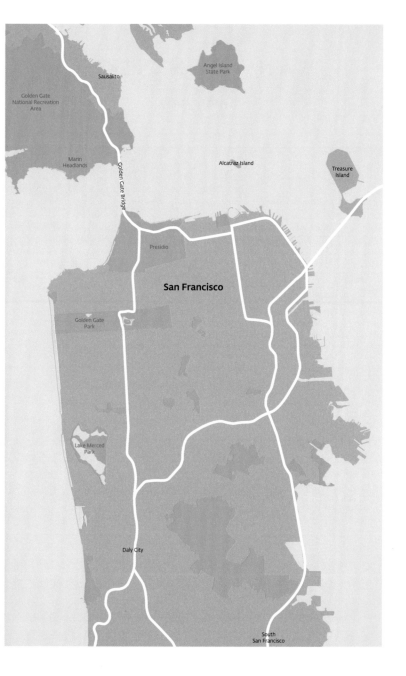

SAN FRANCISCO

overview

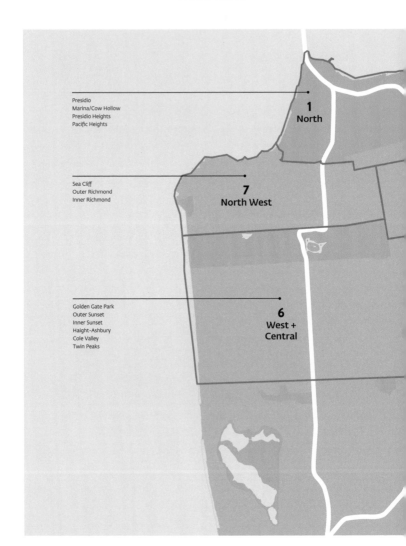

Presidio
Marina/Cow Hollow
Presidio Heights
Pacific Heights

1
North

Sea Cliff
Outer Richmond
Inner Richmond

7
North West

Golden Gate Park
Outer Sunset
Inner Sunset
Haight-Ashbury
Cole Valley
Twin Peaks

6
West +
Central

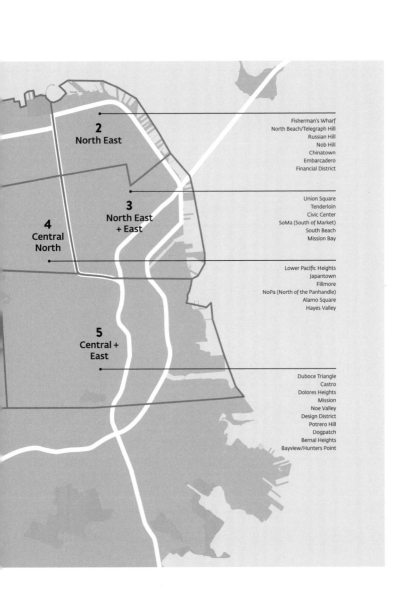

2
North East

Fisherman's Wharf
North Beach/Telegraph Hill
Russian Hill
Nob Hill
Chinatown
Embarcadero
Financial District

3
**North East
+ East**

Union Square
Tenderloin
Civic Center
SoMa (South of Market)
South Beach
Mission Bay

4
**Central
North**

Lower Pacific Heights
Japantown
Fillmore
NoPa (North of the Panhandle)
Alamo Square
Hayes Valley

5
**Central +
East**

Duboce Triangle
Castro
Dolores Heights
Mission
Noe Valley
Design District
Potrero Hill
Dogpatch
Bernal Heights
Bayview/Hunters Point

Map 1
NORTH

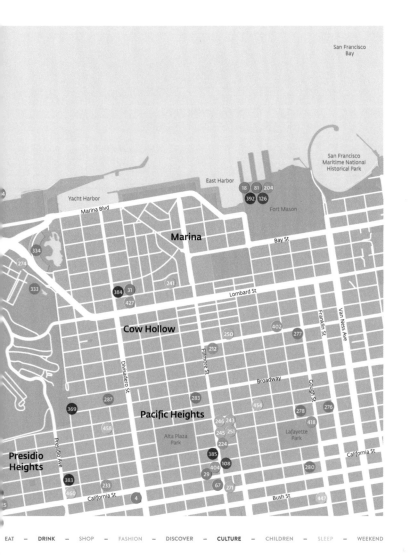

EAT — **DRINK** — SHOP — FASHION — DISCOVER — **CULTURE** — CHILDREN — SLEEP — WEEKEND

Map 2
NORTH EAST

San Francisco Maritime National Historical Park

Fisherman's Wharf

Pier 45

North Beach

Fort Mason

Bay St

Columbus Ave

Pioneer Park

Lombard St

Russian Hill

Washington Square

Telegraph Hill

Van Ness Ave

Union St

Polk St

Robert C Levy Tunnel

Broadway

Chinatown

Nob Hill

Sacramento St

California St

Lafayette Park

Bush St

Pier 39

Stockton St

EAT — DRINK — SHOP — FASHION — DISCOVER — CULTURE — CHILDREN — SLEEP — WEEKEND

Map 3
NORTH EAST and EAST

Map 4
CENTRAL NORTH

Map 5
CENTRAL *and* EAST

EAT — **DRINK** — SHOP — FASHION — **DISCOVER** — **CULTURE** — CHILDREN — SLEEP — WEEKEND

Map 6
WEST and CENTRAL

EAT — **DRINK** — SHOP — FASHION — DISCOVER — **CULTURE** — CHILDREN — SLEEP — WEEKEND

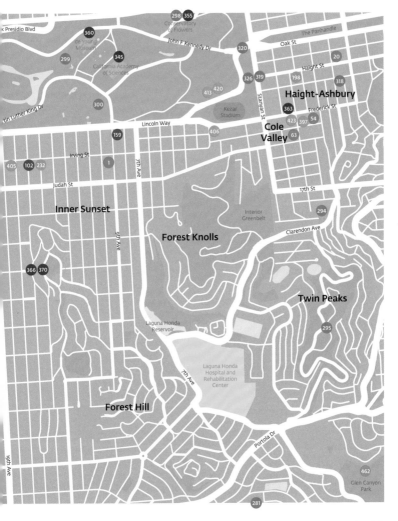

EAT — **DRINK** — SHOP — FASHION — DISCOVER — **CULTURE** — CHILDREN — SLEEP — WEEKEND

Map 7
NORTH WEST

95 PLACES TO EAT OR BUY GOOD FOOD

———

5 of the city's
BEST BAKERIES

1 ARIZMENDI

1331 9th Avenue
Inner Sunset ⑥
+1 415 566 3117
arizmendibakery.com

There is no shortage of options at this worker-owned cooperative bakery – from morning pastries to cookies, and artisan breads to pizza. The latter is on sourdough and it's so good, you should order an extra slice. Get ready to grab one of the brown bags, as you'll be choosing a few things each visit.

2 NEIGHBOR BAKEHOUSE

2343 3rd Street
Dogpatch ⑤
+1 415 549 7716
neighborsf.com

Excellent morning pastries of the sweet and savory kind, as well as sourdough bread loaves. Get there early and get your hands on anything you can (especially the Everything Croissant.) Most things typically sell out way before the 2 pm closing time at this bake shop.

3 JANE THE BAKERY

1881 Geary Blvd
Fillmore ④
+1 415 658 7971
itsjane.com

This is the third location for Jane and where the bulk of the bread-making magic happens. The selections include a wide variety of breads, sweet and savory pastries, while the menu boasts toasts, sandwiches, salads and flatbreads. Head baker Jorgen Carlsen once received 'Best Baguette' and 'Best Croissant' awards.

4   B. PATISSERIE

2821 California St
Pacific Heights ①
+1 415 440 1700
bpatisserie.com

A modern French-style patisserie where seasonal and local influence the offerings, including the famous *kouign amanns,* and new flavors of these are introduced regularly. The wraparound case displays cakes, tarts, macarons and other viennoiserie. For savories they serve tartines and the sister shop across the street offers heartier sandwiches.

5   TARTINE BAKERY & CAFE

600 Guerrero Street
Mission ⑤
+1 415 487 2600
tartinebakery.com

A continuous line forms at this corner bakery – rain or shine. And it's worth the wait each time. Get there early for a morning bun or pain au chocolat. Or stop by at noon for their bread loaves – they are legendary. Their nearby outpost, Tartine Manufactory, offers additional varieties of baked goods, savory dishes and ice cream.

3 JANE THE BAKERY

ancient grains

5 places to satisfy a
SWEET TOOTH

---

6 BOB'S DONUTS

1621 Polk Street
Nob Hill ②
+1 415 776 3141
bobsdonutssf.com

Family-owned since 1960 and open 24 hours daily, which is great because donuts are perfect anytime of the day. They serve good old classics here and they continue to be the best and most affordable in the city. You can also get a BIG ONE that's the size of your face.

7 HOOKER'S SWEET TREATS

442 Hyde Street
Tenderloin ③
+1 415 936 5137
hookerssweet
treats.com

This tiny shop produces small batch, handmade salted caramels with fun names and descriptions for each type. There is the OG (the original, buttery kind) and several others, including the Party Girl packed with all bits of goodness. It is also a cafe and they offer a bread pudding flavor of the day.

8 CRAFTSMAN AND WOLVES

746 Valencia Street
Mission ⑤
+1 415 913 7713
craftsman-wolves.com

The goods here compete for your attention, so take a good look at each case before making your selections. They're known for putting a modern spin on desserts and pastries. A beloved favorite is the Rebel Within, a savory green onions and sausage muffin with a soft-boiled egg hidden inside.

9 **DANDELION CHOCOLATE FACTORY**
2600 16th Street
Mission ⑤
+1 415 349 0942
dandelionchocolate.com

Watch the makers at work at this bean-to-bar, small batch chocolate factory. And while there, enjoy some sweets and drinks in the cafe, or treat yourself to breakfast, afternoon desserts or the prix-fixe chocolate and tea service in the salon. Book a guided tour to complete the experience.

10 **DYNAMO DONUT**
2760 24th Street
Mission ⑤
+1 415 920 1978
dynamodonut.com

Their Maple Bacon donut is a perfect combo of sweet and salty. And all the other inventive flavors they've whipped up are excellent, too. Get here early as they always sell out. This original spot in the Mission has indoor seating and a secret garden space out back.

9 DANDELION CHOCOLATE FACTORY

5 spots for
MEAT LOVERS

---

11 4505 BURGERS & BBQ

705 Divisadero Street
NoPa ④
+1 415 231 6993
4505meats.com

Enjoy plates of smoked meats, like pulled pork, chicken, beef brisket, sausage and ribs, then choose your sides, like the frankaroni and a bag of chicharrones. For a party of 6, order The Presidential which includes all the meats and sides on the menu. Enjoy it all in the outdoor patio or order to-go.

12 HAN II KWAN

1802 Balboa Street
Inner Richmond ⑦
+1 415 752 4447
hanilkwan.org

For Korean barbeque enthusiasts or those wanting to try it, this is the best spot in SF. You can have your meat served pre-cooked, or you can choose to grill it yourself at your table. The latter is the way to go. And enjoy it with all the side dishes brought to your table.

13 COCKSCOMB

564 4th Street
Mission Bay ③
+1 415 974 0700
cockscombsf.com

Chef Chris Cosentino is a master of butchery and he leaves no parts wasted. There are traditional cuts and servings, but the menu offers dishes like beef heart tartare, oven roasted pig's head and the Butcher's Choice, which is a medley of 'fall offs' from the day. Be adventurous. It's all delicious.

14 MARLOWE

500 Brannan Street
Mission Bay ③
+1 415 777 1413
marlowesf.com

One of the best bistro spots with tasty, meaty favorites like their infamous Marlowe Burger, steak tartare, juicy ribeye and bone marrow. And plenty of other non-meat dishes, too – the brown butter Brussels sprouts chips and warm deviled eggs especially. Bright space, brilliant decor, it has the feeling of an ornate little butcher's shop.

15 ROLI ROTI

+1 510 780 0300
roliroti.com

Anytime you see this food truck, head right over. They spit-roast delicious, slow-cooked meats, but it's truly about the porchetta sandwich here. It's piled high with juicy and crispy slices of pork and comes with caramelized onions and arugula. The potatoes absorb the meat drippings and are sprinkled with lavender sea salt. Refer to their website for locations.

5

VEGETARIAN AND VEGAN *restaurants*

16 **CHA-YA VEGETARIAN**
762 Valencia Street
Mission ⑤
+1 415 252 7825

This small vegan and vegetarian Japanese spot has an extensive menu of options, including tempura, gyoza, sushi rolls, rice dishes and noodle options. And plenty of sake to accompany your meal – try a flight. Service is typically quick turnaround and they accept cash only.

17 **GRACIAS MADRE**
2211 Mission Street
Mission ⑤
+1 415 683 1346
gracias-madre.com

Here you'll find tasty Mexican food made solely with organic, vegan, plant-based, non-GMO ingredients. The menu is seasonally focused and based on what's available at their farms. Cheeses and milks are made from nuts. And tortillas and *tamales* are handmade from heirloom corn.

18 GREENS RESTAURANT
AT: FORT MASON,
BUILDING A
2 Marina Boulevard
Marina/Cow Hollow ①
+1 415 771 6222
greensrestaurant.com

This vegetarian focused restaurant is located in one of the historic Fort Mason buildings with sweeping views of the Golden Gate Bridge and waterfront. Open since 1979, they source all their ingredients from their farm in Marin and from other local organic farmers to select the freshest produce to bring to the table.

19 SHIZEN
370 14th Street
Mission ⑤
+1 415 678 5767
shizensf.com

A fully vegan sushi bar and *izakaya* (small dish) restaurant. For those with plant-based diets, the chefs here use ingredients, like tapioca, mountain yam and bean curd, to create tasty, satisfying dishes without having to imitate animal proteins. In addition to sushi and small plates, they offer ramen, too.

20 VEGANBURG
1466 Haight Street
Haight-Ashbury ⑥
+1 415 548 8000
veganburg.com

Introducing the world's first 100% plant-based burger joint. This fast-food chain prides itself on an entirely vegan menu consisting of various burger options that come with a side of seaweed fries or broccoli. They also have a vegan version of chicken tenders and franks and non-dairy soft serve for dessert.

5 *places to*
SLURP OYSTERS

21 **PETIT MARLOWE**
234 Townsend Street
Mission Bay ③
+1 415 923 8577
petitmarlowesf.com

It's charm galore at this Parisian-style wine and oyster bar. The menu includes a raw bar full of oysters and shellfish, caviar, crudos and other small bites of cheese, charcuterie and tartines. Other must-try plates are the tartare and deviled eggs, each served three unique ways. Its sister restaurant is Leo's Oyster Bar.

22 ANCHOR OYSTER BAR

579 Castro Street
Castro ⑤
+1 415 431 3990
anchoroysterbar.com

A charming, locally owned seafood restaurant and market that has been serving city patrons for over 30 years. It's tiny and not ideal for big groups. Put your name on the whiteboard and get ready to wait. The cioppino is a must.

23 HOG ISLAND OYSTER CO.

1 Ferry Building,
Shop 11-A
Embarcadero ②
+1 415 391 7117
hogislandoysters.com

These delicious local oysters are sustainably grown and harvested up north in nearby Tomales Bay, and you can enjoy some here if you can't make it out of the city. Pair a platter with local beer and wine in this stunning location inside the historic Ferry Building along the waterfront.

24 SWAN OYSTER DEPOT

1517 Polk Street
Nob Hill ②
+1 415 673 1101
swanoysterdepot.us

An institution that has been around for 100 years now. It's a fresh fish market, as well as a diner with limited counter seating. Don't let the long line dissuade you though, as it moves quite fast. Most folks are picking up their seafood order or plopping down for a quick bite. Cash only.

25 HOOK FISH CO.

4542 Irving Street
Outer Sunset ⑥
hookfishco.com

Walk in and check out the signs above noting the fresh catches of the day (including oysters), where it originated from, how it was caught and who caught it. These guys are all about sustainable fishing practices and serving tasty snacks, like fish tacos, crab cakes and sandwiches. It's a great spot for a bite by the beach.

5 places to grab a good
PIZZA PIE

---

26 DEL POPOLO

855 Bush Street
Union Square ③
+1 415 589 7940
delpopolosf.com

What started as a mobile pizzeria is now a brick and mortar serving up the same flavorful, naturally leavened, thin crust, wood-fired pizzas. And they've added some inventive sides to accompany your pies. Their massive 6-meter pizza truck (a converted shipping container with a wood-fire oven) continues to pop-up in the city.

27 FLOUR + WATER PIZZERIA

702 Valencia Street
Mission (5)
flourandwater
pizzeria.com

This is the latest spinoff of longtime favorite Flour + Water Restaurant. The focus here is serving five craveable red pies and five white – all available for takeout and delivery. There is a side window for ordering the 'Big Slice' of the day to-go. It is 8 dollars and the size of a half pizza.

28 GOLDEN BOY PIZZA

542 Green Street
North Beach/
Telegraph Hill ②
+1 415 982 9738
goldenboypizza.com

Simple, square-cut, fresh baked focaccia with tasty pizza toppings served here. They offer 4 to 5 basic combos and you can view them all from the window before you order. They're available by the slice or sheet and you can enjoy it at the counter or take it to go. Tip: cash only and yes, order an extra slice.

29 PIZZERIA DELFINA

2406 California St
Pacific Heights ①
+1 415 440 1189
pizzeriadelfina.com

A terrific place for Neapolitan-inspired pizzas and Southern Italian antipasti, pasta, and *piatti*. And perhaps the best Margherita and meatballs in town – these are staples on the menu. Pie toppings and side dishes change based on seasonal ingredients. And breadsticks, freshly grated cheese and stems of herbs are brought to your table.

30 PIZZETTA 211

211 23rd Avenue
Outer Richmond ⑦
+1 415 379 9880
pizzetta211.com

A tiny, unassuming joint with a few tables inside, a couple out front and perfect thin-crust pizzas. They offer several options to choose from each night. The restaurant is tucked along a row of apartment buildings and houses, so expect locals and visitors trying to cram in here. It's so good and so worth it.

5 of the city's
BEST BURGERS

---

31 CAUSWELLS

2346 Chestnut Street
Marina/Cow Hollow ①
+1 415 447 6081
causwells.com

Come here and right away order the burger. It's available from lunch to dinner time. Called the 'Americana', it comes with not one, but two beef patties, gooey melted cheese in between, special sauce and served with a mountain of fried onions on the side. Fries you'll need to order separately.

32 NOPA

560 Divisadero Street
NoPa ④
+1 415 864 8643
nopasf.com

This place is booked every night because it's that good. They serve an all organic cuisine using the best seasonal goodness California offers, and that makes for a good burger. It's grass-fed beef, wood-grilled, topped with pickled onions and served on a house-made brioche bun. A city favorite since they opened.

33 MAVEN

598 Haight Street
Haight-Ashbury ⑤
+1 415 829 7982
maven-sf.com

The secret to Maven's deliciously spiced burger are dashes of Angostura bitters that go right into the meat. Then it's topped with Muenster cheese and house pickles. Even their Juniper-salted fries are amazing. Order the burger during two happy hours Monday to Friday and you get a free Old Fashioned cocktail.

34 SPRUCE

3640 Sacramento St
Presidio Heights ①
+1 415 931 5100
sprucesf.com

The patty here is ground fresh daily and is a mix of brisket, sirloin and short rib. It comes topped with pickled red onion, zucchini, tomato, a caper remoulade and served on an English muffin along with a side of duck fat fries. Is it worth 20 dollars? Yes. You can also add foie gras for another 20.

35 PRAIRIE

3431 19th Street
Mission ⑤
+1 415 483 1112
prairiesf.com

The world is shifting towards plant-based alternatives to protect the environment, so let's add an Impossible Burger to the mix. Here it's charcoal-grilled, served on milk bread with pickled ramp aioli. The add-ons include swiss cheese, grilled avocado and Calabrian XO-fried egg (a medley of dried scallops, shrimps, anchovies and chile). Say yes to all of this.

31 CAUSWELLS

5
GREAT BURRITOS
according to locals

---

36 EL CASTILLITO
136 Church Street
Duboce Triangle ⑤
+1 415 621 3428

Burritos here come packed and heavy. The spit-grilled *al pastor* is especially flavorful on the sweeter side and juicy. But order any and each comes with a big bag of chips to go with all the condiments in the salsa bar. Bring cash or hit the ATM close by before you get here.

37 EL FAROLITO
2779 Mission Street
Mission ⑤
+1 415 824 7877
elfarolitosf.com

Be prepared for a line out the door and potential food coma. The burrito servings are plentiful. The super size of anything can feed two or you save the extra for later. Or try the *suiza*, a giant *quesadilla* packed with tasty meats and other fillings. It's quick, authentic and real tasty Mexican food.

38 LA TAQUERIA

2889 Mission Street
Mission Ⓢ
+1 415 285 7117

A hefty, meat-packed burrito is what you order here. An insider tip: be sure to ask for it 'dorado' style where the tortilla is grilled. It's not mentioned on the menu. There are very long lines and limited seating, so not ideal for big groups. They accept cash only.

39 PAPALOTE MEXICAN GRILL

3409 24th Street
Mission Ⓢ
+1 415 970 8815
papalote-sf.com

A great place to bite into a big burrito and they have really excellent salsa. So good that there are bottles of it that can be purchased to go. And every order comes with a side of it and chips. They also have better seating options here than the other joints.

40 TAQUERIA CANCÚN

2288 Mission Street
Mission Ⓢ
+1 415 252 9560

It's all about the *mojado* (wet) burrito here and it's topped with salsa, melted cheese and sour cream. A fork is required, as you'll want to break into it and soak up the enchilada sauce it comes with. It's all enjoyed with a bag of chips and more salsa.

5 places to get
GOOD DUMPLINGS

41 DUMPLING TIME
11 Division Street
Design District ⑤
+1 415 525 4797
dumplingtimesf.com

This spot puts a trendier spin on traditional dumplings and it's fun and delicious. For example, the King Dum is a super-sized *xiao long bao* (XLB for short) that comes with flower garnishes and a large straw to slurp in the soup. Eat and drink it fast before the skin absorbs all the juices.

42 KINGDOM OF DUMPLING
1713 Taraval Street
Outer Sunset ⑥
+1 415 665 6617
kingofchinese dumpling.com

Stick to the dumplings here. It's a small space, so add your name and party size to the list, wait outside, someone will take your order, and you'll be seated when a table is ready. As soon as you're at your table, those tasty dumplings quickly appear.

43 MAMA JI'S
4416 18th Street
Castro ⑤
+1 415 626 4416
mamajissf.com

The owners share all the tasty Sichuan specialties they grew up with plus daily made dim sum. You choose the level of spiciness for your dishes. And to note, they only offer Belgian beers here. They're open for lunch and dinner and generally there's less of a wait during the earlier times on weekdays.

44 DRAGON BEAUX

5700 Geary Blvd
Outer Richmond ⑦
+1 415 333 8899
dragonbeaux.com

A more modern spin on traditional dumplings here. Many varieties will be ordered and shared, and one will most likely be the colorful Five Guys Xiao Long Bao. Each is tinted using beets, turmeric, squid ink and spinach, then filled with ingredients like pork, kale, crab roe and black truffle.

45 YANK SING

101 Spear Street
SoMa ②
+1 415 781 1111
yanksing.com

Dim sum is served in the traditional style with push carts stopping by your table. Ogle the goods from the steamy containers and platters, then make your selections. And pace yourself, as the carts come often and quickly. The ambiance and prices are more elevated than most, but worth it.

41 DUMPLING TIME

5 *must-visit*
FOOD MARKETS

---

46 BI-RITE MARKET
3639 18th Street
Mission ⑤
+1 415 241 9760
biritemarket.com

One of the best independently owned urban groceries, especially if you care about sustainable, farm-direct, organic freshness, and quality artisan items. The staff is super-friendly and extremely knowledgeable about the products they carry. They also have a great recipe book and ice cream. Grab a scoop or a pint while you're there.

47 NIJIYA MARKET
1737 Post Street
Japantown ④
+1 415 563 1901
nijiya.com

This Japanese market is stocked with the most vibrantly packaged candies, snacks, beverages and condiments. You'll find all kinds of delightful and interesting ingredients from Japan and fresh fish for sushi making. Hit the aisle with grab-and-go sushi, bento boxes and other tasty rice dishes if you need a quick bite.

48 FERRY BUILDING MARKETPLACE
1 Ferry Building
Embarcadero ②
+1 415 983 8030
ferrybuilding marketplace.com

Previously a ferry terminal, it is now a culinary mecca of the best flavors and producers of Northern California. Experience farm fresh produce, prepared meals, packaged foods and handmade goods to fill your kitchens. The best time to visit are Farmers Market days.

49 MISSION COMMUNITY MARKET

Bartlett and
22nd Streets
Mission ⑤
*missioncommunity
market.org*

This vibrant market is held on Thursday evenings from 4 to 8 pm. Farmers, small local businesses and community members convene to promote family health in a fun and festive environment. Enjoy live music and entertainment while you shop. It's a block party.

50 RAINBOW GROCERY

1745 Folsom Street
Mission ⑤
+1 415 863 0620
rainbow.coop

This is a worker-owned cooperative offering an outstanding selection of organic and locally sourced products at fairly reasonable prices. There are bins upon bins of spices and ingredients available in bulk. And the varieties are impressive, including dried and even fermented foods. You may just find foods here you never knew existed.

48 FERRY BUILDING MARKETPLACE

5

CHEESE AND SPECIALTY SHOPS

---

51 CHEESE PLUS

2001 Polk Street
Nob Hill ②
+1 415 921 2001
cheeseplus.com

The cheese counter is at the back of the shop, but there are a great number of gourmet goodies and treats to tempt you up front before you even get there. The cheese variety is impressive and you can pick up everything else you need to accompany them, including wine and chocolates.

52 COWGIRL CREAMERY

1 Ferry Building,
Suite 17
Embarcadero ②
+1 415 362 9354
cowgirlcreamery.com

The actual creamery is located further north of San Francisco, but this is the spot in the city to taste what may be some of the best cheese this region has to offer. Named after iconic Northern California landmarks, Cowgirl offers mainly soft, creamy aged cheeses plus a few fresh ones.

53 THE EPICUREAN TRADER

401 Cortland Avenue
Bernal Heights ⑤
+1 415 872 9484
theepicurean trader.com

A modern day larder of small batch artisan foods and products, craft spirits, wine and fresh goods including cheeses, cured meats, olive oil and flowers. The perfect place to venture for unique chocolates, raw honey, spices and specialty items. They also have a monthly whiskey club and host regular tasting events.

54 SAY CHEESE

856 Cole Street
Cole Valley ⑥
+1 415 665 5020
saycheesesf.com

Family-owned and operated since 1976, this tiny cheese and wine shop sources many great varieties from around the world. So much goodness is packed into this space. They can prepare platters and cheese boards for your gatherings, and they're also the go-to spot for the best sandwiches in the neighborhood.

55 SALUMERIA

3000 20th Street
Mission ⑤
+1 415 471 2998
salumeriasf.com

This shop offers a great variety of house-made charcuterie, cheese, pantry essentials and a daily selection of freshly made pastas from sister restaurant Flour + Water. A chalkboard menu lists the sandwiches and salads of the day. Also a perfect spot for a quick bite – rain or shine – as they have an enclosed patio.

5 restaurants where
DINING MAKES A DIFFERENCE

56 **FIORELLA**
   2339 Clement Street
   Outer Richmond ⑦
   +1 415 340 3049
   fiorella-sf.com

Owner Boris Nemchenok grew up in SF, and his love for the city is shown on the walls (featuring the most iconic people and places in the Bay Area), and in the way he gives back to the community. 10% of sales from a select pizza on the menu supports a local elementary school's art program.

57 **OLD SKOOL CAFE**
   1429 Mendell Street
   Bayview/Hunters
   Point ⑤
   +1 415 822 8531
   oldskoolcafe.org

This youth-run, jazz-themed supper club serves as a job training and violence prevention program for youth aged 16 to 22 years. Family recipes they've grown up with are transformed into inspiring and delicious comfort dishes. Youth artists provide live entertainment on Thursday, Friday and Saturday evenings.

58 MOZZERIA

3228 16th Street
Mission ⑤
+1 415 489 0963
mozzeria.com

A pizzeria with a purpose. It is owned by deaf couple, Russell and Melody Stein, and operated by only deaf individuals. The business includes this brick and mortar, two food trucks, and next year, a larger restaurant in Washington, DC. Simply sign, point or write your order, and enjoy their delicious Neapolitan pizzas.

59 FLOUR + WATER

2401 Harrison Street
Mission ⑤
+1 415 826 7000
flourandwater.com

Not only is it a great restaurant, it hosts a number of fundraisers each year to support a local high school and also relief efforts following natural disasters. They will soon host a guest chef series where a portion of proceeds benefit a local charity of the chef's choice. Follow their social media for updates.

60 DELANCEY STREET RESTAURANT

600 The Embarcadero
South Beach ③
+1 415 512 5179
delanceystreet
foundation.org

Since 1991, this restaurant has been operated by those who've hit rock bottom and are eager to make a positive difference. They are residents of Delancey Street, a self-help organization that provides former inmates, substance abusers and gang members with work and skills they need to lead better lives.

5 great
BRUNCH SPOTS
worth waiting for

---

61 **MAMA'S ON WASHINGTON SQUARE**

1701 Stockton Street
North Beach/
Telegraph Hill ②
+1 415 362 6421
mamas-sf.com

Perhaps the most iconic breakfast spot in the city which has been serving for over fifty years. Select from many omelettes, benedicts and other egg dishes, then order some of their fresh baked goods with some homemade jam. Look for the long line forming around the corner of the park.

62 **PLOW**

1299 18th Street
Potrero Hill ⑤
+1 415 821 7569
eatatplow.com

Arguably one of the top spots for weekend brunch and breakfast – and rightfully so. Breakfast here is so good it's served all day throughout the week. Get the lemon ricotta pancakes on top of anything you decide to order. And do expect a wait during peak times; you won't be disappointed.

63 **ZAZIE**

941 Cole Street
Cole Valley ⑥
+1 415 564 5332
zaziesf.com

Brunch is everyday here and the egg options are tremendous and endless. There are over five different kinds of pancakes and french toast to choose from, too. They're available in servings of one, two or three pieces. Now you get why it's so popular?

64 **PRIMAVERA**

AT: FERRY PLAZA
FARMERS MARKET
1 Ferry Plaza
Embarcadero ②
+1 707 939 9350
primaveratamales.com

This may be the best breakfast or brunch you'll find at this farmers market. It also happens to be the stand with the longest line. Folks eagerly wait for their plate of fresh, organic *tamales*, tacos and *chilaquiles*. The latter is the crowd favorite each time. Saturdays only from 8 am to 2 pm.

65 **OUTERLANDS**

4001 Judah Street
Outer Sunset ⑥
+1 415 661 6140
outerlandssf.com

A warm, woodsy spot for a comfy meal anytime of the day – especially in this often chilly and foggy part of the city. Think thick cast iron-grilled cheese sandwich and Dutch pancakes. Expect long lines for weekend brunch, but they have parklets outside where you can hang out and catch up with friends over coffee.

5 restaurants with
BEAUTIFUL INTERIORS

---

66 **LEO'S OYSTER BAR**

568 Sacramento St
Financial District ②
+1 415 872 9982
leossf.com

Perhaps the most photographed is this elegant cocktail and raw oyster bar with a tropical, garden-themed setting and the lushest palm wallpaper. Everyone asks about it. If you make a dinner reservation, you may get seated in the beautiful hidden Champagne Room in the back. And beyond that is another little hidden tiki bar.

67 **NOOSH**

2001 Fillmore Street
Pacific Heights ①
+1 415 231 5985
nooshsf.com

It feels as if you've escaped on a short vacation away from SF, then came right back. Very Eastern Mediterranean meets Californian. That vibe is felt throughout the stylish space and the menu, which include kebabs, flatbreads and spreads. After all, in Farsi, *noosh* means lovely and joy felt from good food and company.

68 **VILLON**
AT: SAN FRANCISCO
PROPER HOTEL
1100 Market Street
Tenderloin ③
+1 628 895 2040
properhotel.com

Hire Los Angeles-based Kelly Wearstler, interior designer *extraordinaire*, and the space will surely be magic. Think early pre-modernist European style combined with SF's artsy and eclectic vibe. Enjoy excellent shareable plates along with any of the 7×7 cocktails (yes, 49 of them) from the dining room or lounge.

69 **WAYFARE TAVERN**
558 Sacramento St
Financial District ②
+1 415 772 9060
wayfaretavern.com

A very handsome establishment with decorative dining rooms, banquettes and bars on multi levels. The walls are adorned with trophy heads and giant urns are bursting with florals – it's very huntsman chic. You'll enjoy spectacular comfort dishes (like their famous fried chicken) and warm popovers are brought to your table.

70 **MOURAD**
140 New
Montgomery St
SoMa ③
+1 415 660 2500
mouradsf.com

An exquisite Moroccan establishment, from the food to the ambiance, set within a historic art deco building. The food is innovative (a fusion of Californian and Moroccan) and the interior is superbly decorative. Choose your own dishes or be wonderfully surprised by the chef's tasting menu. It's a classy joint so dress sharp for this one.

5 *great*
DATE NIGHT
spots

---

71 KOKKARI ESTIATORIO
200 Jackson Street
Financial District ②
+1 415 981 0983
kokkari.com

Cozy, candlelit and consistently excellent Greek comfort dishes. A perfect place to enjoy a memorable meal and someone's company. The menu is filled with mezes, so plenty to order and share throughout the night. The *saghanaki* (pan fried cheese with lemon) is a must.

72 ZUNI CAFE
1658 Market Street
Hayes Valley ④
+1 415 552 2522
zunicafe.com

One of the city's beloved favorites. It's perfect for small bites, especially from the raw bar, and comfort dishes, like it's famous Chicken for Two. Order as soon as you get seated, as it takes 60 minutes to prepare. Enjoy the caesar salad, shoestring fries and some wine until it arrives.

73 COTOGNA
490 Pacific Avenue
Financial District ②
+1 415 775 8508
cotognasf.com

Pasta is cozy and comforting and this is a great date spot – for the ambiance and the excellent rustic Italian fare. The menu, which also includes wood-fired pizzas and spit-roasted meats, is seasonal so perhaps you'll discover new dishes together. Or pop in for their delicious Sunday Supper.

74 LIHOLIHO YACHT CLUB

871 Sutter Street
Lower Nob Hill ③
+1 415 440 5446
lycsf.com

Flavorful, Hawaiian-inspired dishes with favorites like poke on a seaweed crisp, beef tongue buns and the Baked Hawaiian, which you must save room for at the end. There's also the hidden Louie's Gen Gen Room below with a different small bites and cocktail menu. The open kitchen is central and the chef's mother smiles from behind the bar.

74 LIHOLIHO YACHT CLUB

75 RICH TABLE

199 Gough Street
Hayes Valley ④
+1 415 355 9085
richtablesf.com

Husband-and-wife team, Evan and Sarah Rich, have combined their years cooking at the most premier restaurants to offer a seasonally driven menu of California's finest ingredients. Each dish is a surprising mix of flavors and the result is delicious. Try the sardine woven into a potato chip served with horseradish crème fraiche.

5 *fun*
PLAY DATE
spots

---

76 STEM KITCHEN & GARDEN

499 Illinois Street
Potrero Hill ⑤
+1 415 915 1000
stemkitchensf.com

A great farm-to-table rooftop restaurant with an outdoor garden and patio, firepits, bocce ball court and sweeping views of the bay. It's a perfect spot to play bocce anytime of the day. They're open Monday to Friday (with Happy Hour from 3 to 6 pm) and on Saturday for brunch.

77 EMMY'S SPAGHETTI SHACK

3230 Mission Street
Bernal Heights ⑤
+1 415 206 2086
emmysspaghetti shack.com

As the name alludes, expect heaping plates of pasta along with vibrant decor, music, games and a photo booth. It's a fun vibe here and it is generally packed with families, kids and folks having a good time later in the evenings. This place is boisterous and entertaining.

78 FOREIGN CINEMA

2534 Mission Street
Mission ⑤
+1 415 648 7600
foreigncinema.com

The perfect all-in-one spot for dinner and a movie. Or weekend brunch. It's a stunning multi-room restaurant that projects films against the central patio wall. And it's perfect for a date night. The fare includes a raw bar of oysters and California-inspired cuisine. Film screenings are announced on their website.

79 **MISSION BOWLING CLUB**

3176 17th Street
Mission ⑤
+1 415 863 2695
*missionbowling
club.com*

A boutique bowling alley with six lanes that also serves comfort food for dinner, as well as cocktails, beer and wine. They're also open for weekend brunch. Insider tip: they have one of the city's best burgers. Book ahead for a lane or dining table and let's hope you strike with your date. For ages 21 and over.

80 **URBAN PUTT**

1096 South
Van Ness Avenue
Mission ⑤
+1 415 341 1080
urbanputt.com

A miniature golf course plus food and drinks – always a good time. It's perfect for all ages and it's also indoors. There are 14 holes to play and each round incorporates some cool tech and fun design. It is housed in an old Victorian and there is a full-service restaurant and bar on the second level.

5 places to catch a
FOOD TRUCK

---

81 OFF THE GRID
AT: FORT MASON
CENTER PARKING LOT
2 Marina Boulevard
Marina/Cow Hollow ①
+1 415 339 5888
offthegrid.com

On Friday nights, crowds convene here with over a dozen food truck options, a band and other live performances. These occur during the Spring to Fall months when the weather is warmer. As it is located by the waterfront, be sure to wear extra layers and maybe bring a blanket.

82 PRESIDIO PICNIC
IN FRONT OF: WALT
DISNEY MUSEUM
104 Montgomery St
Presidio ①
+1 415 561 5300
presidio.gov/food

During the warmer months and on Sunday only, pack some blankets and lawn chairs and head to the Presidio for this massive daytime lawn party. There are a great number of trucks offering food and drinks. Plus the location offers perfect views of the Golden Gate Bridge and waterfront.

**83 SOMA STREAT
FOOD PARK**
428 11th Street
SoMa ③
*somastreat
foodpark.com*

It's called a culinary carnival and urban playground, as there are food trucks, booze, carnival games, TVs and Wi-Fi. Lots to entertain you while you eat. This one is also open daily and you can check the schedule online to preview the food options. They also host trivia nights here.

84 SPARK SOCIAL SF

601 Mission Bay
Boulevard North
Mission Bay ③
sparksocialsf.com

An urban gathering place that combines food trucks, a beer garden and events. It is open throughout the week for lunch and dinner and there are special happy hours Monday to Saturday. The food truck options change each day, so be sure to check the online calendar.

85 OFF THE GRID

5th and Minna
Streets
SoMa ③
+1 415 339 5888
offthegrid.com/event/
5-m-5th-minna

Rain or shine, plenty of food trucks line up inside the tunnel for this one. It is held every Wednesday and Friday from 11 am to 2 pm and serves the downtown crowd. Visit the website to see which trucks will be popping up.

82 PRESIDIO PICNIC

5 great
SPIN-OFF
RESTAURANTS

---

86 TACOS CALA
50 Hickory Street
Hayes Valley ④
calarestaurant.com

Just behind big sister Cala Restaurant and down an alley is this small, standing room only *taquería*. Open Monday to Friday from 11 am to 2 pm, it's a great spot to get a quick bite from one of the city's best female chefs. Guacamole and chips, *aguas frescas* and *horchata* are also available.

87 RT ROTISSERIE
101 Oak Street
Hayes Valley ④
+1 415 829 7086
rtrotisserie.com

Quick, tender, juicy, tasty rotisserie chicken brought to you by the fine folks behind city favorite, Rich Table restaurant. Choose either a half or a whole with a couple of sauces, then order up some tasty side dishes. Sandwiches and one salad is offered on the menu.

88 MOONGATE LOUNGE
28 Waverly Place
Chinatown ②
moongatelounge.com

Fans of Mister Jiu's can now flock to this lounge located a floor above the restaurant. Six house cocktails, six seasonal cocktails (inspired by the Chinese lunar calendar), and small bites are offered on the menu. A reservation is required, and seating is time-limited based on your party size.

89 PETIT CRENN

609 Hayes Street
Hayes Valley ④
+1 415 864 1744
petitcrenn.com

A more approachable, seafood-forward tasting menu from Chef Dominique of Atelier Crenn. The ambiance is cozy, modern and features an open kitchen. The seafood and vegetable dishes combine French classics with Northern California ingredients. No meat is served and service is included in the menu prices.

90 LOUIE'S GEN-GEN ROOM
AT: LIHOLIHO YACHT CLUB

871 Sutter Street
Nob Hill ②
+1 415 440 5446
liholihoyachtclub.com/
gengen

Walk all the way through the restaurant, then down the stairs to find this little sibling of Liholiho Yacht Club. It is a tropical-like cocktail bar with its own small bites and drinks menu. The grilled cheese with black truffles and honey butter is incredible.

5 good old
CLASSIC SF JOINTS

---

91 CLIFF HOUSE

1090 Point Lobos
Sea Cliff ⑦
+1 415 386 3330
cliffhouse.com

Dine inside one of the oldest and most picturesque landmarks in SF. The original Cliff House (erected in 1863) burned down and has been rebuilt numerous times since. Today you can still look out towards the ocean and see the ruins of the famous Sutro Baths below. The perfect spot to watch the sunset.

92 THE OLD CLAM HOUSE

299 Bayshore Blvd
Bayview/
Hunters Point ⑤
+1 415 826 4880
theoldclamhousesf.com

This is the city's oldest restaurant which has proudly served in the same location since 1861. The bar area consists of the original structure. Every guest is given a shot of hot clam juice to start their meal and the menu offers classic seafood dishes like cioppino, chowder and fish and chips.

93 ST. FRANCIS FOUNTAIN

2801 24th Street
Mission ⑤
+1 415 826 4210
stfrancis
fountainsf.com

Introducing SF's oldest ice-cream parlor and diner open since 1918. They offer an extensive menu of good old classics and local-inspired dishes for breakfast and lunch, as well as ice-cream scoops, splits and sundaes. Feel like you stepped back in time. And vegan options now available – as it is SF.

94 TADICH GRILL

240 California Street
Financial District ②
+1 415 391 1849
tadichgrill.com

When it comes to traditional, authentic
SF, this place comes to mind for many.
It is one of the city and state's oldest
restaurants and looks as it did 160 years
ago. They are famous for their seafood –
especially the cioppino – and their broiled
meats. No reservations, expect to wait and
guaranteed your meal will be great.

95 TOMMY'S JOYNT

1101 Geary Boulevard
Fillmore ④
+1 415 775 4216
tommysjoynt.com

A landmark in the city known for
real hearty meat platters and hefty
sandwiches. Think roast beef, corned
beef and juicy brisket. All kept nice and
warm under heat lamps, ready to be
sliced and served. The ambiance is dark
and kitschy and there is a large bar for
beer and beverages.

92 THE OLD CLAM HOUSE

TRICK DOG

80 PLACES
FOR A DRINK

5
CULT COFFEE
shops of SF

---

96 BLUE BOTTLE KIOSK
315 Linden Street
Hayes Valley ④
+1 510 653 3394
bluebottlecoffee.com

This coffee company was founded by James Freeman, who sought a lightly roasted cup to expose the beans' natural flavors, similar to Japan where baristas slowly brewed each by hand. He opened this tiny kiosk in 2005 and the masses loved it. Today there are several Blue Bottles located in the city.

97 PHILZ
3101 24th Street
Mission ⑤
+1 415 875 9370
philzcoffee.com

No espresso drinks here. For 25 years it's been all about brewing one cup at a time and customizing it to your preference (milk type and sweetness level). They offer over twenty blends of beans, all listed on the large menu board. This is the original location of the first Philz.

98 LINEA
3417 18th Street
Mission ⑤
lineacaffe.com

This is the boutique roaster's first location with a much larger roastery and cafe slated to open soon. *Food & Wine* magazine included Linea in its lineup of the 11 Best Indie Coffee Shops in America, and its sweet coffee blends are absolutely deserving of that title.

99 **ANDYTOWN**

3655 Lawton Street
Outer Sunset ⑥
andytownsf.com

This is where Andytown started, and then it added a roastery, training lab and another cafe further out in the neighborhood. The latest outpost is downtown inside Facebook's building. Fans have flocked to their locations for great coffee and their signature drink called the Snowy Plover.

100 **SIGHTGLASS COFFEE**

3014 20th Street
Mission ⑤
+1 415 641 1043
sightglasscoffee.com

Two brothers founded this cafe and roastery which takes its name from the viewing window on their vintage PROBAT Roaster. They source their green coffee from many regions and operate as small-batch producers, allowing them to perfect their methods.

100 SIGHTGLASS COFFEE

5

PICTURE PERFECT
SPACES *for coffee*

---

101 20TH CENTURY CAFE
198 Gough Street
Hayes Valley ④
+1 415 621 2380
20thcenturycafe.com

This place is reminiscent of a charming little coffee shop you'd find in Eastern Europe. Every detail is delightful – from the design and decor to the serving pieces. Not to mention fabulous lunch dishes (like *borscht* and a *reuben*) and desserts (*babka*, *knish* and *tortes*). I highly suggest a slice of the Russian Honey Cake.

102 HOLLOW
1435 Irving Street
Inner Sunset ⑥
+1 415 242 4119

It's like walking into a woodsy wonderland full of delightful gifts, coffee and locally made sweets. And such a cozy spot to hide out in for just a little bit. The husband-and-wife team of this cafe also run the sweet home shop next door called Dandy.

103 LE MARAIS
498 Sanchez Street
Castro ⑤
www.lemarais
bakery.com

This is Le Marais' third location in the city and it's the prettiest of them yet. Lovely and light filled and oh so Parisian! There's a 'Bonjour' as soon as you step through the door. It's a boulangerie and patisserie that serves espresso, coffee, as well as heartier options for lunch and dinner.

104 LADY FALCON COFFEE CLUB

Parked near Hayes and Steiner Streets
Alamo Square ④
+1 415 606 1884
ladyfalcon
coffeeclub.com

Find this darling, vintage-truck-driving-barista parked at Alamo Square Friday to Sunday from 9.30 am to 3 pm. A great cup of coffee in the most pictured spot in SF – you can't top that. Or you may happen upon it at another surprise location in the city.

105 TARTINE MANUFACTORY

595 Alabama Street
Mission ⑤
+1 415 757 0007
tartinebakery.com/san-
francisco/manufactory

This expansive, light-filled space serves as a restaurant, bakehouse, ice-cream counter and cafe. The coffee stand is in the middle and you can watch all the goodness happening around you while you wait, including their breadmaking. And be sure to pick up a loaf; they're famous for it.

101 20TH CENTURY CAFE

5 *great*
COFFEE SHOPS
TO GET WORK DONE

---

106 BEACON COFFEE & PANTRY

805 Columbus Ave
North Beach/
Telegraph Hill ②
+1 415 814 2551
beacon-sf.com

Located on the quieter edge of North Beach is this terrific cafe (and market) where you can plug in and get some work done. It's airy with plenty of seating, Wi-Fi, great natural light and it has a living succulent wall that adds a refreshing and soothing vibe to the space.

107 CAFE ST. JORGE

3438 Mission Street
Bernal Heights ⑤
+1 415 814 2028
cafestjorge.com

Head to this Bernal cafe for a little taste of Portugal in the city. There is plenty of seating, but if you need to power up the laptop, score a table to your left. And stay and work awhile, as they offer a tasty California/Portuguese-inspired menu of organic breakfast and lunch dishes.

108 JANE ON FILLMORE

2123 Fillmore Street
Pacific Heights ①
+1 415 931 5263
itsjane.com/location/
jane-on-fillmore

A cozy spot for working solo for a short period. However, it's a bakery and cafe serving excellent pastries, all-day breakfast, and lunch dishes, so it's worth parking here for a bit. There is additional seating in the mezzanine above.

109 THE SOCIAL STUDY

1795 Geary Blvd
Fillmore ④
+1 415 292 7417
thesocialstudysf.com

In the evenings, it's a lounge for winetails, beertails and soju cocktails. Daytime starting at noon, bring your laptop, enjoy free Wi-Fi and get some work done. Snacks and lunch can be ordered until 3 pm and board games are available if you need a fun break.

110 VERVE COFFEE ROASTERS

2101 Market Street
Castro ⑤
+1 415 780 0867
vervecoffee.com/pages/
market-street

Although limited seating, Verve is full of natural light, offers communal tables, free Wi-Fi and remarkable coffee. Expect it will be crowded at peak times, like most cafes. Their food menu is served daily from 7 am to 2 pm.

5 places to
SIP TEA

———————

111 LOVEJOY'S TEA ROOM

1351 Church Street
Noe Valley ⑤
+1 415 648 5895
lovejoystearoom.com

A frilly and fun space with mismatched tea sets, linens, and vintage furnishings. In fact, it used to be an antique shop and has since evolved into the tearoom it is now. They also have a shop across the street with antique serving pieces and tea blends for purchase to host your own gathering.

112 SONG TEA & CERAMICS

2120 Sutter Street
Japantown ④
+1 415 885 2118
songtea.com

A simple and elegantly designed gallery and tasting room with rare, exceptional quality teas and wares (tea pots and cups) mainly from China and Taiwan. Guests are invited to sit, taste, chat, browse and unwind. Porcelain jars contain an ever changing selection of teas discovered by the shop owner during his travels.

113 SAMOVAR TEA BAR

411 Valencia Street
Mission ⑤
+1 415 553 6887
samovartea.com

Modern and minimal describes this perfect spot for just tea. The menu consists of select blends that can be ordered to-go or enjoyed onsite. Their housemade chai is exceptional – piping hot, rich, full of spice and blended in big copper pots. There's even a vegan version, too.

114 THE ROTUNDA

150 Stockton Street
Union Square ③
+1 415 249 2720
neimanmarcus.com/
restaurants

Atop the Neiman Marcus department store is this elegant restaurant situated under a stained-glass dome with a view of Union Square. They're open daily from 11 am to 4 pm for lunch and the beautiful afternoon tea service (with exquisite sweets, cookies, tarts and finger sandwiches) starts at 2 pm.

115 STONEMILL MATCHA

561 Valencia Street
Mission ⑤
+1 415 796 3876
stonemillmatcha.com

This is the city's first premium matcha cafe serving lattes, cold brews and sweets infused with the fine green tea powder from the Kyoto region of Japan. For the full dining experience, hearty Japanese comfort dishes, like the *katsu sando*, are available. They've partnered with SF's best bakeshops to create their pastries and desserts.

5 of the best places for
CRAFT COCKTAILS

---

116 **ABV**

3174 16th Street
Mission ⑤
+1 415 400 4748
abvsf.com

This popular neighborhood bar is open daily and early starting at 2 pm until 2 am. Drinks are organized by spirit making it easy to peruse the selections. Bites and snacks are listed on the menu board, but you'll need to eat it all with your hands as they offer no flatware.

117 **TRUE LAUREL**

753 Alabama Street
Mission ⑤
truelaurelsf.com

It's no wonder this bar has some of the best cocktails and bar snacks in town. The team emerged from Lazy Bear, the highly regarded, multi Michelin star supper club in SF. The cocktail concoctions will surely surprise you, like floating drops of shiso oil or an added sprig of freshly foraged pine needles.

118 **HORSEFEATHER**

528 Divisadero Street
NoPa ④
+1 415 817 1939
horsefeatherbar.com

Simply a good neighborhood bar with good throwback cocktails, which can be enjoyed in the plant-filled atrium that serves as the entrance, or in the moodier, mid-century styled main room. One of the secret ingredients in their cocktails: house-made syrups made with wine, sugar, herbs and fruits.

119 LOLÓ

974 Valencia Street
Mission ⑤
+1 415 643 5656
lolosf.com

Reimagined and uniquely inspired Mexican food and drink using local ingredients are the focus here. Their Agave Bar is stocked with some of the best mezcal and tequila selections, which are blended into their cocktails. They make a terrific margarita. And they serve until midnight on Friday and Saturdays.

120 TRICK DOG

3010 20th Street
Mission ⑤
+1 415 471 2999
trickdogbar.com

Continuously the best, most inventive cocktails in the city. They introduce a new menu every six months, each uniquely themed and presented in many forms – from record holders to story books. Get in early as it packs a crowd. And be sure to order some bites, like the Trick Dog.

5 places for
COCKTAILS IN
A LUXE SETTING

---

121 **THE BIG 4**
1075 California St
Nob Hill ②
+1 415 771 1140
big4restaurant.com

This place has retained its old world charm and has the ambiance of a gentlemen's club. In fact, The Big 4 is a nod to four legendary men of the Pacific Coast railroad history who lived in lavish mansions surrounding the restaurant. Dress sharp. There is a dress-code for dinner, but it's more casual in the lounge.

122 **COMMONS CLUB**
AT: VIRGIN HOTELS
SAN FRANCISCO
250 4th Street
SoMa ③
virginhotels.com/
san-francisco

Find this lavish bar within the Virgin Hotel lobby and enjoy cocktails and meals within its opulent rooms, filled with leather and velvet seating. It's every bit of style you would expect from the Virgin Group. Floor-to-ceiling windows further light up the space and exquisite chandeliers drip from the ceiling.

123 THE SARATOGA

1000 Larkin Street
Tenderloin ③
+1 415 932 6464
thesaratogasf.com

Snag a seat at the stunning back-lit bar at this chic, bi-level cocktail lounge and restaurant in the Tenderloin. The cocktail menu includes a great variety of highballs, barreled, bottled, shaken and stirred recipes, as well as an impressive 100 dollar 'Cocktail Bill' Boothby Bowl to be shared amongst a group.

124 COLD DRINKS BAR

644 Broadway
Chinatown ②
+1 415 788 8188
chinalivesf.com

There is no visible sign, so upon arrival head up the steps and follow the bats to this hidden cocktail cave. You'll feel as if you stepped into another era with its vintage glam vibe and tuxedo-clad bartenders. The menu focuses on scotches and scotch cocktails. Their signature drink is an Old Fashioned with duck fat.

125 BIX

56 Gold Street
Financial District ②
+1 415 433 6300
bixrestaurant.com

You'll feel as if you stepped into the 1920s in this fine establishment, though it really opened in 1988. It's tucked within the old brick buildings of the Barbary Coast enclave. Belly up to the mural-scaped bar, get seated for dinner on the floor or balcony, and watch live jazz performances nightly.

5

BEER HALLS *and* BEER GARDENS

---

126 RADHAUS
AT: FORT MASON CENTER
Landmark Building A
Marina/Cow Hollow ①
+1 415 445 4556
radhaussf.com

This modern Bavarian-styled beer hall is situated by the water with a view of the Golden Gate Bridge. A picturesque place to savor over a dozen drafts, bottles, cocktails and wine over brunch, lunch or dinner. Food menu items include oysters, pretzels, bratwursts and schnitzels.

127 BIERGARTEN
424 Octavia Street
Hayes Valley ④
+1 415 252 9289
biergartensf.com

Head to this fun, outdoor German beer garden at the very heart of Hayes Valley. It always packs a crowd, so save any seat you see available, order up at the counter and head to your table. Great selection of beers and fare like pretzels, sausages and sliders. Sister restaurant Suppenküche is across the way.

128 STANDARD DEVIANT BREWING
280 14th Street
Mission ⑤
+1 415 590 2550
standarddeviant brewing.com

Not your average beer hall. It's a fun, casual warehouse space filled with picnic tables, pinball machines, shuffleboard and board games. They have a small menu of their tasty beers and offer up very light snacks, like popcorn and potato chips. Come here for good vibes and good beer.

129 MIKKELLER BAR SF

34 Mason Street
Union Square ③
+1 415 984 0279
mikkellerbar.com

This Danish beer hall has 42 beers on tap including 4 exclusive to this location. Each is controlled by a crazy machine called the 'Flux Capacitator' (remember *Back to the Future*?) that maintains their compound levels. A room dedicated to sour beers is open on weekends. No flights here; taste a couple first or go all in with your selection.

130 SCHROEDER'S

240 Front Street
Financial District ②
+1 415 421 4778
schroederssf.com

This Bavarian-style beer hall has served the city for over 120 years. The original was destroyed in the 1906 earthquake and fire, then reopened in its current location. Order up some American and German beers by the glass, in a boot or as a flight. The menu takes a modern spin on *pretzels*, *wursts* and *schnitzels*.

5 unique
WINE BARS

131 **TERROIR**
1116 Folsom Street
SoMa ③
+1 415 558 9946
terroirsf.com

Specializing in natural and organic wines from around the globe (especially France), the selections here are unique and ever-changing. At first glance it feels like you stepped into a cool coffee shop, but it's not. It's a great laidback spot to enjoy good music, small bites and interesting wine.

131 TERROIR

132 MISSION CHEESE

736 Valencia Street
Mission ⑤
+1 415 553 8667
missioncheese.net

There are many cheese varieties to choose from at this cheese and wine bar. Or you can be adventurous and order the 'cheesemonger's flight'. Mention what types you like and they'll surprise you with some of their yummy selections. They offer great wines to pair with all of them.

133 VERJUS

528 Washington St
Financial District ②
+1 415 944 4600
verjuscave.com

The latest favorite addition to SF is this French-inspired wine bar, bistro and bottle shop. The wine bar offers a few communal tables and a selection of small plates listed on a chalkboard menu. Sit-down dinner can be enjoyed in the adjoining space where nightly dishes are highlighted above the kitchen.

134 THE RIDDLER

528 Laguna Street
Hayes Valley ④
+1 415 589 7002
theriddlersf.com

An exquisite little champagne bar to celebrate life's joyous occasions. It is backed entirely by a team of women and there are sweet feminine touches in the decor and the menu offerings. They offer an extensive list of bubbly from around the globe and complimentary popcorn bar with a station of flavorful seasonings.

135 UNION LARDER

1945 Hyde Street
Russian Hill ②
+1 415 323 4845
unionlarder.com

A beautiful, high-ceiling wine bar with excellent cheese, charcuterie and small plates. It's also a mini market of gourmet pantry items and ingredients. Although it's situated on the cable car line, it's cozy and charming, as it's tucked within a quiet neighborhood. Their tiny sister shop, Little Vine, is in North Beach.

5

LOCAL WINERIES

that don't require a visit to wine country

---

136 BLUXOME STREET WINERY

53 Bluxome Street
Mission Bay ③
+1 415 543 5353
bluxomewinery.com

This working winery brings California winemaking back to where it originally started (not in Sonoma or Napa like most of us thought). In fact this SoMa region was home to over a hundred wineries and cellars – most destroyed by the 1906 earthquake or shut down by prohibition. Today it's a perfect spot to try some excellent wines – most notable are their Pinot Noirs.

137 DOGPATCH WINEWORKS

2455 3rd Street
Dogpatch ⑤
+1 415 525 4440
dogpatch
wineworks.com

This urban winery allows you to make a custom barrel of wine from start to finish and offers tastings of small batch wines produced right on the premises. A fantastic option, especially if you want to avoid the drive and traffic out to the wine regions. It's also a stunning event space.

138 ERISTAVI WINERY

1300 Potrero Avenue
Potrero Hill ⑤
+1 415 578 0599
eristaviwinery.com

Looks are deceiving and you'll be surprised to find this hidden gem in this neighborhood. This winery and tasting room has a hip warehouse feel and they offer generous pours of their wines along with a small menu of cheese and charcuterie to taste with your pairings.

139 JAX VINEYARDS

326 Brannan Street
South Beach ③
+1 415 446 9505
jaxvineyards.com

This winery produces their wine in Napa Valley but you can sample their entire portfolio here at this tasting room in the city. It also has an outdoor area with a fire pit and heat lamps. They offer happy hour specials and terrific cheese plates.

140 TANK18

1345 Howard Street
SoMa ③
tank18.com

Seasonal wines are sourced from local wine regions and brought back to the city in metal tanks. Here at the tasting room you can order these wines by the glass, bottle or as a flight. They also host a monthly bring-your-own-bottle event where they can be refilled with select wines and labeled at a special rate.

5
LOCAL BREWERIES
to visit

141 **BAREBOTTLE BREWING**

1525 Cortland Ave
Bernal Heights ⑤
+1 415 926 8617
barebottle.com

A cool brewery with cool names for their beers, like Honey Boo Boo or Tart Side of the Force. There is an abundance of tables, shuffleboard, ping-pong and corn hole. You can bring in your own food and there's typically a food truck there, too. They also offer brewery tours and home brewing classes.

141 BAREBOTTLE BREWING

142 BLACK SANDS BREWERY

701 Haight Street
Haight-Ashbury ④
+1 415 534 5194
blacksandsbeer.com

A place for beer, bites and supplies to make your own brew at home. You can watch them make it, taste it, see the recipe and leave with everything to make the beer yourself. There are no secrets to their process here. You can also sign up for their homebrewing classes.

143 CELLARMAKER BREWING COMPANY

1150 Howard Street
SoMa ③
+1 415 863 3940
cellarmaker
brewing.com

This small brewery is continuously experimenting with hops, grains, barrels and yeasts, so new limited brews are often introduced. And that makes it fun for them and folks visiting. They offer a good mix so there's something for everyone. It's a small space with very limited seating.

144 HARMONIC BREWING

1050 26th Street
Dogpatch ⑤
+1 415 872 6817
harmonicbrewing.com

Located in a warehouse in the city's Dogpatch is this tasting room where you can see the beers brewed in front of you. They have 12 beers on tap available as tasters, full pours or in growlers to-go. There is typically a food truck or vendor outside to offer bites with your beer.

145 ANCHOR BREWING

1705 Mariposa Street
Potrero Hill ⑤
+1 415 863 8350
anchorbrewing.com

This brewery has been operating in the city since 1896. Join a tour, visit the vats, then finish with a tasting in their original taproom. Across the street is Public Taps where you can order beer daily from noon to evening time. They host food trucks and events in this space.

LOCAL DISTILLERIES

to visit

146 HOTALING & CO.

1705 Mariposa Street
Potrero Hill ⑤
+1 415 863 8350
hotalingandco.com

Formerly known as Anchor Distilling, this tasting room is one of the few places you can sip spirits on an open rooftop while enjoying gorgeous views of the city. America's first craft gin post-prohibition was created right here just over ten years ago by founder, Fritz Maytag.

147 SEVEN STILLS DISTILLERY

1439 Egbert Avenue,
Unit C
Bayview/
Hunters Point ⑤
+1 415 914 0936
sevenstillsofsf.com

A beautiful industrial space on the far edge of the city that has not one, but two bars: one for beer and another for whiskey. Pick your poison or try both. It's a unique brewery and distillery that makes beer, whiskey made from craft beers, vodka and bitters.

148 HANGAR 1 VODKA

2505 Monarch Street
Alameda
+1 510 871 4950
hangarone.com

This distillery is located in an actual WWII-era hangar in nearby Alameda. They work with farmers sourcing seasonal fruits to produce their line of vodkas – or farm-to-hangar, as they call it. You can schedule a tour of their facility or head straight into their gorgeous tasting room.

149 DISTILLERY NO. 209
AT: PIER 50, SHED B
401 Terry Francois
Boulevard
Mission Bay ③
+1 415 369 0209
distillery209.com

The only distillery built over water keeping the temperature right for distilling year-round. Originally established in 1882 at a winemaking facility in Napa, the new property owners discovered its history with plans to restore it, but its size and location weren't ideal to revive it. It now sits on the Bay where folks can visit and enjoy it.

150 ST. GEORGE SPIRITS
2601 Monarch Street
Alameda
+1 510 769 1601
stgeorgespirits.com

Technically not in San Francisco, but very close and worth a visit as it's one of the best makers of small batch gin, vodka, whiskey, bourbon, absinthe, rum, fruit brandies and flavored liqueurs. They have a massive facility on a former naval base and you can sign up to tour the stills, fermentation tanks and barrels.

150 ST. GEORGE SPIRITS

SPECIALTY SPIRITS BARS

151 MOSTO

741 Valencia Street
Mission ⑤
+1 415 649 6077
mostobar.com

Tequila and mezcal are focal here. They serve craft cocktails with these agave spirits paired with a smaller menu of Mexican street food. Big sister restaurant, Tacolicious, is next door and you can wait here until your table is ready.

152 RICKHOUSE

246 Kearny Street
Financial District ②
+1 415 398 2827
rickhousebar.com

Whiskey is king and they have ceiling-high shelves full of them. So high and wide they need a rolling ladder to get to them. The ceiling is also made of barrel staves from Kentucky. Squeeze into one of the bar stools for drinks or sneak upstairs to get a good look at the space.

153 HARD WATER

Pier 3
Embarcadero ②
+1 415 392 3021
hardwaterbar.com

A stunning American whiskey bar that beautifully displays its bottle collection. A sliding ladder is required to reach most of them. Belly up to the wraparound bar and enjoy your whiskey the way you like it, or sample new varieties as a flight. New Orleans-inspired bites complete the menu.

154 SMUGGLER'S COVE

650 Gough Street
Fillmore ④
+1 415 869 1900
smugglerscovesf.com

This award-winning tiki bar is dedicated to all things rum and cocktails inspired by eras, regions and other legendary tiki bars. Many hard-to-find rums can be experienced here. The menu has over 80 recipes. Power through them (with a stamp card to prove it) and you will be rewarded.

155 WHITECHAPEL

600 Polk Street
Tenderloin ③
+1 415 292 5800
whitechapelsf.com

Calling all gin lovers. Find 400 varieties of the spirit and 120 gin-based cocktails at this joint. The ambiance is reminiscent of a Victorian-era distillery set in an abandoned underground London train station. Even the food menu, consisting of hearty English fare, is designed to look like an old train schedule.

5 fun bars with
OUTDOOR PATIOS

---

156 ANINA
482 Hayes Street
Hayes Valley ④
aninasf.com

A fun, lively bar with island-inspired cocktails, spritzes and large group-size punch bowls. There is plenty of seating, most notably the outdoor patio full of picnic tables. Get there early to score seats. No food here but occasionally they'll have a pop-up food vendor offering bites.

157 ARGUELLO
50 Moraga Avenue
Presidio ①
+1 415 561 3650
arguellosf.com

This restaurant with an enclosed outdoor patio and a fire pit is hidden in the Presidio Officers' Club. Perfect spot to escape the frenzy of the city and enjoy some tasty Mexican bites and margaritas. Especially if you're exploring the Presidio, this is a good place to unwind for a bit.

158 SOUTHERN PACIFIC BREWING

620 Treat Avenue
Mission ⑤
+1 415 341 0152
*southernpacific
brewing.com*

This brewery has ample seating in the front patio, within the entrance and on the second level. The massive space is open and airy and filled with plants and trees – it feels like the outdoors from within. Check the chalkboard for the daily house brews and guest beer options.

159 NOPALITO

1224 9th Avenue
Inner Sunset ⑥
+1 415 233 9966
nopalitosf.com

In this chilly part of town, it sure helps to have outdoor seating with heat lamps. And Nopalito serves exceptional organic Mexican cuisine to enjoy with cervezas and cocktails with mezcal and tequila. An order of the *totopos con chile* is a must for every meal, especially if you're enjoying rounds of drinks here.

160 VIRGIL'S SEA ROOM

3152 Mission Street
Bernal Heights ⑤
+1 415 829 2233
virgilssf.com

This funky nautical-inspired bar on the outer edge of the city has a fantastic outdoor heated patio with an ocean blue mural, too. It's the perfect chill spot and typically not overcrowded given its distance. The bar has an easy cocktail menu plus all your standard booze. Also it's cash only.

5 great
ROOFTOP BARS

---

161 **CHARMAINE'S**
AT: SAN FRANCISCO
PROPER
1100 Market Street
Tenderloin ③
+1 415 786 3467
charmainessf.com

This rooftop lounge and cocktail bar sits atop the hip, new Proper Hotel. A great beverage program paired with gorgeous design. The line starts at a separate entrance adjacent to the main one of the hotel, then you're escorted to a small elevator. The fire pits will keep you warm on chilly nights.

162 **DIRTY HABIT**
AT: HOTEL ZELOS
12 4th Street
SoMa ③
+1 415 348 1555
dirtyhabitsf.com

Find this bar on the fifth floor of Hotel Zelos. There are no city views, but it has great outdoor space with a large central fire pit. Reserve ahead for a table outside. They offer punch bowls to share, shot and beer pairings and a great number of seasonal, stirred and shaken cocktails.

163 **JONES**
620 Jones Street
Lower Nob Hill ③
+1 415 496 6858
620-jones.com

It's only on the second story, but this massive rooftop bar gives you a good view of downtown and the surrounding neighborhood. Plus they have three bars: two inside and one on the open terrace decked with palms and string lights. This is a hot happy hour spot, too.

164 **EL TECHO**
2516 Mission Street
Mission ⑤
+1 415 550 6970
eltechosf.com

Head to this rooftop bar, not just for a glass, but a pitcher of margaritas. You'll be here for a while. There are various styles to choose from along with flavorful Mexican bites. Enjoy views of the Bay Bridge, downtown and the surrounding Mission. Even better, catch the sunset from here.

165 **EVERDENE**
AT: VIRGIN HOTELS
SAN FRANCISCO
250 4th Street,
12th Floor
SoMa ③
+1 415 534 6500
virginhotels.com/san-francisco

This is the latest rooftop bar that debuted in the city. Even at 12 stories, you get tremendous views of SF from this indoor and outdoor cocktail lounge and restaurant. The space can be protected from the elements, so it's a wonderful, tropical-inspired place to enjoy any day.

161 **CHARMAINE'S**

5 great bars where
TIME STANDS STILL

---

166 DOGPATCH SALOON
2496 3rd Street
Dogpatch ⑤
dogpatchsaloon.com

Opened in 1912 and just over 100 years old. The space has been redesigned with much vintage appeal, but the actual bar and stained glass windows have been retained. A good spot for drinks only – it's casual, no frills and plenty of seating. It's also dog-friendly so you might see plenty of pups.

167 THE HOMESTEAD
2301 Folsom Street
Mission ⑤
+1 415 282 4663
homesteadsf.com

This neighborhood bar was opened in 1906 as the 'Old Homestead' and probably kept much of the same decor that was around during the turn of the century. It resembles a Victorian-style parlor with its pressed tin ceiling and nudie paintings. Drinks are cheap and reasonable and peanut shells crunch under your feet.

168 HOUSE OF SHIELDS
39 New Montgomery Street
SoMa ③
thehouseofshields.com

Open since 1908, this bar is all about tradition. No TVs or clocks in here. Just a handsome, ornate space serving some good old classic drinks. Belly up to the bar or reserve a booth or spot in the upper mezzanine. It's a tad dark and musky up there – as it should be.

169 COMSTOCK SALOON

155 Columbus Ave
Chinatown ②
+1 415 617 0071
comstocksaloon.com

Serving as a watering hole for San Francisco since 1907, this space has retained even the original trough that runs along the bottom edge of the bar. It's a beautiful spot to enjoy some classic, well-crafted cocktails and live music nightly. The blue-tiled side is called the Monkey Bar. See how many monkeys you can spot here.

170 THE SALOON

1232 Grant Avenue
North Beach/
Telegraph Hill ②
+1 415 989 7666

Opened in 1861, it's the oldest saloon in the city and it looks and smells like it. Attracting all walks of life and playing live jazz each night – it's fantastic. All your standard alcohol and cheap beers are offered here and it's cash only. Ask for a fancy drink and you'll get rejected.

169 COMSTOCK SALOON

5

SECRET SPEAKEASY BARS

---

171 HIDEOUT

3121 16th Street
Mission ⑤
+1 415 252 7740
dalvasf.com/hideout

Perhaps you're over the Mission crowds and looking for a quiet spot to retreat for a drink? Find Dalva, head towards the back and step into the Hideout. It's intimate, dimly lit and a perfect bar for beer and craft cocktails with no more than a friend or two.

172 MARIANNE'S

360 Jessie Street
SoMa ③
+1 415 321 6000
mariannessf.com

Book ahead to access this small hidden bar named after Mick Jagger's famous ex, Marianne Faithfull. The decor is inspired by her sixties bohemian style with ambient music and card games to entertain you. Cocktails have names like 'Honey Bang Me Sloe' and 'Sticky Fingers' which can be ordered as individuals or as a 'commune' for six.

173 LINDEN ROOM

330 Gough Street
Hayes Valley ④
+1 415 829 7565
nightbird
restaurant.com

The entrance is down an alley with an unmarked door – bit hard to find if you don't know what you're looking for. It's tied to Nightbird restaurant to help guide you a bit. Once in, it seats no more than a dozen people and offers just a few well-crafted cocktails.

174 THE REMEDIE ROOM

256 Columbus Ave
North Beach/
Telegraph Hill ②
+1 415 766 4363
thedevilsacre.com/
remedie-room

Go see the 'doctors' for apothecary-inspired remedies in the hidden room below The Devil's Acre. Libations and elixirs have been expertly crafted to help you celebrate or cure your troubles. It's open Friday and Saturday evenings and seats at most 30 people.

175 BOURBON & BRANCH / WILSON AND WILSON PRIVATE DETECTIVE AGENCY

501 Jones Street
Tenderloin ③
+1 415 346 1735
bourbonand
branch.com

Make a reservation to get the password to enter this establishment tucked away in the Tenderloin. Once in, you'll be greeted and seated in one of the 'secret' booth rooms to begin your cocktail experience. If you don't have a reservation, you can enter around the corner to access their public bar called The Library.

JOSHU+VELA

60 PLACES TO SHOP

5 shops featuring
LOCAL ARTISTS
and MAKERS

176 THE VOYAGER SHOP
365 Valencia Street
Mission ⑤
+1 213 995 9951
thevoyagershop.com

In addition to stylish men and women's clothing and accessories, Voyager features goods and homeware designed by local artists and makers, like canvas totes from SF's Joshu+Vela and jewelry from Oakland favorite Marisa Mason. They also host monthly pop-ups to feature individual collections.

177 GRAVEL & GOLD
3266 21st Street
Mission ⑤
+1 415 552 0112
gravelandgold.com

This gem is owned by a collective of creative women who stock their handmade wares, as well as those of other local artists and makers. You'll find jewelry, fragrances, kitchenware, books and other gifts, but what they're most known for are their clothing, accessories and bedding with bold and playful prints.

178 RARE DEVICE
600 Divisadero St
NoPa ④
+1 415 863 3969
raredevice.net

A fantastic shop and art gallery filled with unique and nifty gifts for big people and little ones, too. Many local and independent designers' pieces are on display here. And each month there is an exhibit of a local artist's work in the space.

179 FOGGY NOTION

124 Clement Street
Inner Richmond ⑦
+1 415 683 5654
foggy-notion.com

This shop showcases the work of designers and artists from San Francisco and beyond. Products are handmade, organic and environmentally-conscious, including leather bags and wallets, home goods, jewelry and art. Many are made by shop proprietress, Alissa Anderson.

180 INDUSTRIOUS LIFE

1095 Tennessee St
Dogpatch ⑤
+1 415 349 3479
industriouslife.com

If you're seeking small furnishings, lighting, textiles, ceramics, jewelry and objects created by some of the city's talented designers and makers, you'll find a good collection here at this shop in the Dogpatch. There are also some vintage design pieces thrown into the mix, as we all tend to live with a bit of old and new.

178 RARE DEVICE

5 great
MADE IN SF
shops

---

181 BRYR STUDIO

2331 3rd Street
Dogpatch ⑤
+1 415 374 7323
bryrstudio.com

Maker of modern and chicly-designed clogs inspired by West Coast stylish living. Each pair is handmade by a small team on site in your size, silhouette and color using traditional European wooden bases and high-quality American leathers. This process takes over thirty days from start to finish, so place your order sooner rather than later.

182 HEATH CERAMICS

2900 18th Street
Mission ⑤
+1 415 361 5552
heathceramics.com

Makers of handcrafted ceramic dinner-ware and tiles for homes, restaurants, and hotels since 1948. This location in the Mission includes a beautiful showroom, a tile factory, gallery, newsstand and artist studios upstairs. To get an inside look, sign up for a tour and see areas not accessible to the general public.

181 **BRYR STUDIO**

183 TIMBUK2

587 Shotwell Street
Mission ⑤
+1 415 321 6806
timbuk2.com

This factory store is blocks from the garage where it all began 30 years ago. The founder, a former bike messenger, loved the functionality and utility of a messenger bag, and wanted it to be more accessible to many. The classic messenger bag was born, and the line has expanded to more quality bags since.

184 JOSHU+VELA

3042 16th Street
Mission ⑤
+1 415 872 5347
joshuvela.com

Stylish, practical, lasting and locally made. These canvas and leather utility bags and accessories are crafted with your everyday use in mind. This studio and showroom is where you can see all the products and observe how they're made. It is a small-team, small-batch production process and only the best materials and utter care go into every item.

185 YONDER SF

701 11th Avenue
Inner Richmond ⑦
+1 650 303 9216
yondershop.com

This space serves as Linda Fahey's studio where she handbuilds her iconic vessels and sculptures, as well as retail space where the work of her many talented artist friends is showcased. She teaches and hosts workshops throughout the year.

5
VINTAGE SHOPS
for cool finds

---

186 **BELLE COSE**
CLOTHES & INTERIOR
2036 Polk Street
Nob Hill ②
+1 415 474 3494

It's as if three storefronts were combined into one, as they have three separate spaces for women's items, men's and a home section. The selections are almost entirely vintage with a few new pieces thrown into the mix. There are plenty of treasures to be found on every surface and in the cases and cubbies.

187 **JONATHAN RACHMAN DESIGN**
INTERIOR
1632-C Market Street
Hayes Valley ④
+1 415 440 1234
jonathanrachman.com

Jonathan Rachman travels the globe designing interiors while collecting beautiful objects to take back home, especially ones that are centuries old and have special stories behind them – he'll fill you in on those tales. The shop is a trove of treasures, full of all the lovely things he has amassed and everything is for sale. A gorgeous space to peruse and admire.

188 LOCAL STRANGE
FURNITURE

3243 Balboa Street
Outer Richmond ⑦
+1 415 737 5415

The fellows here are always on the hunt for cool stuff, most of which is local and collected from homes and garages in the neighborhood and the surrounding areas. And their prices are super decent, too. The items to really score here are the chairs – lots of mid-century ones, especially original and classic Eames kinds.

189 THE PERISH TRUST
INTERIOR

728 Divisadero St
NoPa ④
theperishtrust.com

A curated trove of old flags, paintings, books, typewriters, tools, trophies, nautical gadgets, and other rare American knick knacks. Many new items like jewelry, bags, artwork, decor and books are offered, too. The back is the owners' kitchen stocked with locally handmade crafts.

190 CAROUSEL CONSIGNMENT
FURNITURE – INTERIOR –
CLOTHING

2391 Mission Street
Mission ⑤
+1 415 821 9848
carouselsf.com

The two shop owners met at Burning Man and soon learned they shared a love of the circus and all things vintage. Their shop contains a fun and whimsy mix of antiques, furniture, art, decor and clothing they've amassed and found over the years.

5 unique
SPECIALTY SHOPS

---

191 TINA FREY DESIGNS
HOMEWARE

1485 Bancroft Ave
Bayview/Hunters
Point ⑤
+1 415 223 4710
tinafreydesigns.com

Tina Frey designs an elegant and playful collection of homeware using colored resin. Each design is hand sculpted in clay first, then cast. Products include dinnerware, serving dishes, ice buckets, planters and tables. Her studio is impressive and it's where you can preview and purchase her collection.

192 GOOD VIBRATIONS
SEX TOYS

603 Valencia Street
Mission ⑤
+1 415 503 9522
goodvibes.com

A lack of resources for accurate sex information and quality sex toys for women led Joani Blank to open this shop in 1977. It has since added products and services for men, too. It's a safe and welcoming place – much like a bookshop – where you can peruse and ask questions about all products available. They host workshops, too.

193 THE RIBBONERIE
RIBBONS

3695 Sacramento St
Presidio Heights ①
+1 415 626 6184
ribbonerie.com

Satins, silks, velvets, grosgrain, taffeta, sheers, jacquards, stripes, dots and so many more! This delightful little shop is filled with over a thousand spools of ribbons and other notions from around the world. It's the perfect spot to find any kind of ribbon for all your projects.

194 SCHEIN & SCHEIN
MAPS
1435 Grant Avenue
North Beach/
Telegraph Hill ②
+1 415 399 8882
scheinandschein.com

A treasure full of maps can be found here. From local to global, the collection is astonishing. Many are rare and hard-to-find. Cubbies are organized by region or interests, but just tell Jimmie and Marti what you're looking for and they'll guide you in the right direction. Or peek around, as there's plenty to intrigue you.

195 TIGERLILY PERFUMERY
PERFUMES
973 Valencia Street
Mission ⑤
+1 415 896 4665
tigerlilyperfumery.com

The shop features a splendid collection of fragrances from niche, harder-to-find perfumeries from around the world and some made locally in California and San Francisco. Explore and experience the many fragrances on your own or allow shop owner Antonia to expertly guide you on a journey to find the perfect scent.

195 TIGERLILY PERFUMERY

5
CURIOSITY SHOPS
for cool discoveries

---

196 826 VALENCIA

826 Valencia Street
Mission ⑤
+1 415 642 5905
826valencia.org/store

A pirate shop with cubbies full of nifty treasures and nautical knick-knacks. The organization behind it, founded by author Dave Eggers, offers free programs to help young students develop their creative writing skills in a fun and unique environment. They publish books, magazines and newspapers showcasing the impressive work of these aspiring young writers.

197 PAXTON GATE

824 Valencia Street
Mission ⑤
+1 415 824 1872
paxtongate.com

A delightfully bizarre space filled with skeletons, fossils, taxidermy of the exotic kind, carnivorous plants, terrariums, insects, and other random curiosities. It's so creepy and so cool at the same time. You can easily spend hours inspecting and handling every item in there.

198 LOVED TO DEATH

1681 Haight Street
Haight-Ashbury ⑥
+1 415 551 1036
lovedtodeath.com

Skeletons, trophy heads, old embalming tools, Medusa door knockers, jewelry made out of teeth, and specimens in lucite are just some of the creepy little things you'll discover at this quirky shop in the Haight. There's plenty more and worth a peek for curiosity sake. No photos allowed.

199 BELL'OCCHIO

10 Brady Street
SoMa ③
+1 415 864 4048
bellocchio.com

This hidden gem feels as if you stepped into a quaint French village shop. The proprietress carries the loveliest mix of paper goods, stationery, cards, spools of vintage ribbon, chic home goods and other rare gift items. There are sweet little treasures hidden in every cubby in the shop – so be sure to open every one of them.

200 MODERN RELICS

771 Cabrillo Avenue
Inner Richmond ⑦
+1 415 422 0477
alixbluh.
squarespace.com

A delightful little wonderland of decorative items and unique jewelry. Owner and designer, Alix Bluh, makes all her reliquary pieces in the studio space above the shop, drawing inspiration from nature as well as timeless and treasured objects. She custom-makes pieces that are sacred and sentimental to individuals.

5 places to fill up on
ART SUPPLIES

201 THE AESTHETIC UNION

555 Alabama Street
Mission ⑤
theaestheticunion.com

The front serves as a shop for art supplies, stationery and a gallery featuring work by owner James Tucker and other printmakers. The back is the production area for designing and letterpress printing. They also offer workshops. James, an avid sailor, designed the front counter using an old boat.

202 ARTIST & CRAFTSMAN SUPPLY

555 Pacific Avenue
Financial District ②
+1 415 931 1900
artistcraftsman.com

A fantastic employee-owned shop for all your artsy, crafty needs and it's also the site of the former beloved Hippodrome dance hall during the city's raucous Barbary Coast days. Many features of the club still remain. Peruse the aisles for supplies, explore old photos and scope out the tunnel in the basement for a doorway to its past.

203 CASE FOR MAKING

4037 Judah Street
Outer Sunset ⑥
caseformaking.com

This place stocks raw materials (papers, cloths, smocks) and supplies (pens, pencils, paints, brushes and more) for your creative pursuits. They also host a variety of workshops, like watercolor painting, natural dyeing and sketchbook stitching.

204 FLAX ART & DESIGN
AT: FORT MASON

2 Marina Boulevard,
Building D
Marina/Cow Hollow ①
+1 415 530 3510
flaxart.com/
san-francisco-store

Opened in 1938, this is San Francisco's oldest art supply business and it is still family-owned to this day. It has moved to multiple locations throughout the city, but the flagship now resides in Oakland. The shop in SF sits on the beautiful waterfront and continues to carry the best supplies for your projects.

205 SCRAP

801 Toland St
Bayview/
Hunters Point ⑤
+1 415 647 1746
scrap-sf.org

If you have the patience and lots of room for creativity, check this place out. It is a trove of cheap arts and crafts supplies, raw materials and random bits that you'll need to sort through. SCRAP's mission is to repurpose these items for creative use and reduce what goes into landfills.

203 **CASE FOR MAKING**

5

BOOKSHOPS FOR BOOKWORMS

---

206 BLACK BIRD BOOKSTORE

4033 Judah Street
Outer Sunset ⑥
+1 628 256 0081
blackbirdbooksf.com

This isn't your average book shop. The selections are more minimal and mostly focused on current topics, subjects and local interests, so there is a continuous rotation. They also stock some of the latest fiction and non-fiction books, too. The back has a great wooden play and reading area for kids.

207 GREEN APPLE BOOKS

506 Clement Street
Inner Richmond ⑦
+1 415 387 2272
greenapplebooks.com

One of the best independent bookstores selling new and used books, magazines, and other nifty items. Enjoy the sound of the creaky wooden floorboards as you browse the ceiling-high stacks, then hide out in one of the nooks and dive into the pile of books you've gathered.

208 OMNIVORE BOOKS ON FOOD

3885-A Cesar Chavez Street
Noe Valley ⑤
+1 415 282 4712
omnivorebooks.com

This dear little bookshop is solely dedicated to cooking, growing, and just loving food. They carry a vast selection of new and vintage recipe books and magazines. Many chefs and authors make guest appearances and sign their books here, so be sure to check the calendar to see who might be popping in next.

209 CITY LIGHTS BOOKSTORE

261 Columbus Ave
Chinatown ②
+1 415 362 8193
citylights.com

Head here for the books and the history. Founded in 1953 by poet Lawrence Ferlinghetti, it is a landmark independent bookstore and publisher specializing in world literature, arts, and progressive politics. It also happens to be the bookshop that put famous beatnik writers like Jack Kerouac in the spotlight.

210 WILLIAM STOUT ARCHITECTURAL BOOKS

804 Montgomery St
Financial District ②
+1 415 391 6757
stoutbooks.com

As a practicing architect, Bill Stout frequented Europe bringing back hard-to-find architectural books plus extra copies for friends. That became the start of his bookshop, and thirty years later he continues to carry titles dedicated to architecture, art, urban planning, graphic and industrial design, furniture, interiors and landscapes. You'll find his shop in Jackson Square.

206 BLACK BIRD BOOKSTORE

5 *spots for*
SPECIALTY MAGAZINES

211 SMOKE SIGNALS

2223 Polk Street
Russian Hill ②
+1 415 292 6025

The name of the place suggests tobacco products are sold, along with an impressive selection of mass circulated magazines, newspapers, glossy quarterlies, annuals, and foreign editions. They're all tightly packed and organized, and the owners are happy to help if you need assistance.

212 JUICY NEWS SF

2181 Union Street
Marina/Cow Hollow ①
+1 415 441 3051

Local and international magazines and periodicals of all subjects fill the first level of this shop. They have a wonderful collection of coffee table books which are displayed in the second floor nook. And greeting cards are stocked aplenty in case you're purchasing items as gifts.

213 FOG CITY NEWS

455 Market Street
SoMa ②
+1 415 543 7400
fogcitynews.com

This shop carries the largest selection of magazines and periodicals in the Bay Area. Its foreign publications section has over 700 titles from more than 25 different countries. Beyond that it has a vast collection of premium chocolates from around the globe and some pretty nice (and dare I say, naughty) greeting cards, too.

214 HEATH NEWSSTAND

2900 18th Street
Mission ⑤
+1 415 873 9209
heathnewsstand.com

The maker of ceramics (*heathceramics.com*) also has a newsstand stocking local, national and international newspapers, magazines and journals covering many interests. Additionally you can pick up beverages, snacks, candy and small stationery items. There is also a florist on site if you need to pick up some blooms.

215 KINOKINUYA

Japan Center
1581 Webster Street
Japantown ④
+1 415 567 7625
usa.kinokuniya.com

It's a Japanese bookshop, but there is a broad range of selections, magazines, music and gift items to delight anyone. A lot of things are in English. A great spot to preview the latest in Japan's pop culture and aesthetics. If you're hardcore into manga, there is a massive section for it.

5 places for the
BEST BLOOMS

---

216 AMPERSAND
80 Albion Street
Mission ⑤
+1 415 654 0776
www.ampersandsf.com

A darling floral studio and store with the brightest blue door. The sweet owners, Emerson and Benjamin, converted an old garage into their dream space, then filled it with seasonal blooms from local farmers and repurposed vessels for their arrangements. Trust that everything coming out of this place will be perfect for your occasion.

217 SAN FRANCISCO FLOWER MART
640 Brannan Street
SoMa ③
+1 415 392 7944
sanfranciscoflower
mart.com

This mart takes up almost an entire square block and is filled with all sorts of stem flowers, plants, containers and accessories. It's open Monday through Saturday and the early morning hours are reserved for wholesalers with badges, but after 10 am the general public can stop by and shop.

218 BELL AND TRUNK FLOWERS
1411 18th Street
Potrero Hill ⑤
+1 415 648 0519
bellandtrunk.com

A sweet floral shop with arrangements perfect for all your occasions. They also offer other little gifts like candles, perfumes, soaps, salves and lip balms. Everything is arranged against a vibrant green backdrop. Contact Vanessa and she will bundle up beautiful things for you.

219 FARMGIRL FLOWERS

+1 855 202 3817
farmgirlflowers.com

This team sources the freshest blooms from local growers, then designs beautiful arrangements each day at various price points. Orders are placed online. The bouquets are bundled in burlap, then delivered by bicycle or scooter. You're getting a gorgeous arrangement, supporting local farmers and minimizing the impact on the environment.

220 THE PETALER

773 14th Street
Duboce Triangle ⑤
+1 415 335 2205
thepetalersf.com

The lovely studio of designer Rebekah Northway where she arranges the exquisite displays seen in many of the city's restaurants and design spaces. She also drives a sweet flower truck. Her studio is usually closed to the public, but on Fridays you can visit it from 1 to 7 pm to purchase blooms for yourself or a special someone.

216 AMPERSAND

5 unique
HOME DECOR
shops

---

221 FIELD THEORY

3600 Lawton Street
Outer Sunset ⑥
fieldtheorydesign.com

Interior designer Leah Harmatz's space serves as her studio and shop, where you can peruse and purchase her beautiful finds from 11 am to 5 pm on Fridays and Saturdays. Her aesthetic and collection stem from her belief that everyone should have a beautiful, peaceful space to call home.

222 THE HUMAN CONDITION

3148 22nd Street
Mission ⑤
+1 415 658 7580
humanconditionsf.com

An exquisite home decor and lifestyle shop filled with handcrafted items from near and far. Plenty of design books to peruse through, too. But the shop's pièce de résistance: the scenic French wallpaper that draws you in and pulls it all together.

223 COUP D'ETAT

111 Rhode Island
Street, Suite 1
Design District ⑤
+1 415 241 9300
coupdetatsf.com

For serious design enthusiasts and collectors, visit this gallery for things truly extraordinary. The curated collection includes rare, one-of-a-kind vintage, antique items, and pieces from artisans around the world. Every piece is a statement. This place is worth a gander, even if only for inspiration.

224 **NEST**

2300 Fillmore Street
Pacific Heights ①
+1 415 292 6199
nestsf.com

Everything lovely, whimsy, and worldly you'll find here – both vintage and new. Mother and daughter, Judy and Marcella, explore the globe and antique markets in search of unique gift items and treasured pieces to fill their shop. Step inside and feel like you've been transported on a beautiful adventure.

225 **ST. FRANK**

3665 Sacramento St
Presidio Heights ①
+1 415 416 6918
stfrank.com

The studio offers a vibrant selection of handmade decorative pieces using artisan textiles from over twenty countries around the world. Each unique item comes from a special place and with a special story. The store is dedicated to supporting economic empowerment for artisans (through jobs, training and support) and preserving traditional craft.

225 ST. FRANK

5 shops for
COOL SURF and
COASTAL LIVING

226 MOLLUSK SURF SHOP

4500 Irving Street
Outer Sunset ⑥
+1 415 564 6300
mollusksurfshop.com

You don't have to be a surfer to appreciate this spot. The space alone is very colorful and crafty. They stock a mix of surf boards, gear, books, films, prints, clothing and what I think are some of the coolest and comfiest tees out there. There's also an art gallery within.

227 WISE SURFBOARDS

800 Great Highway
Outer Richmond ⑦
+1 415 750 9473
wisesurfboards.com

This local institution has served the surf community since 1968. They have the largest selection of surfboards, wetsuits and gear and have a reputation for excellent service. They stock some used gear as well. You also get a good view of the beach from here.

228 GENERAL STORE

4035 Judah Street
Outer Sunset ⑥
+1 415 682 0600
shop-generalstore.com

Beautiful handmade crafts from West Coast designers are stocked here along with vintage frocks and Levi's. But one of the best features of the shop is the patio out back. It features a garden and greenhouse full of cacti and succulents.

229 WOODSHOP

3725 Noriega Street
Outer Sunset ⑥
woodshopsf.com

Make an appointment to see this
workspace and showroom occupied
by four artists and craftsman whose work
embody the spirit of California living.
One makes wooden surfboards, another
builds furnishings from locally salvaged
hardwoods, the third reinvents chairs in
a cool new way, and the last is a designer
and painter of words on objects and paper.

230 GENERAL STORE HOME

3928 Irving Street
Outer Sunset ⑥
+1 415 682 7100
shop-generalstore.com

Its sister shop is located several blocks
away and this newest addition features
a wider collection of ceramic dinner-
ware, kitchenware, decorative pieces
and furnishings for the home. For the
ultimate relaxed California vibe, this
is your destination.

226 MOLLUSK SURF SHOP

5 shops to
STOCK YOUR KITCHEN

---

231 COOKIN'

339 Divisadero Street
NoPa ④
+1 415 861 1854

There is barely enough room to maneuver this store, but just let owner Judy know what you're looking for. The place is teeming with every cooking and kitchen tool you can imagine. Everything is previously owned and ready for a new home and prices are very reasonable.

232 DANDY

1433 Irving Street
Inner Sunset ⑥
+1 415 326 3911
dandy-life.com

Located right next door to Hollow (the cafe she owns with her husband) is interior designer Dawn Kirker's home goods shop. The tiny, light filled space is full of sweet home scents, simple kitchenware, gadgets, serving pieces and stationery. A particular favorite are the glass salt and pepper shakers with animal heads.

233 MARCH

3075 Sacramento St
Pacific Heights ①
+1 415 931 7433
marchsf.com

Elegant cookware, tools and pantry goods for the more refined kitchen. And always a beautiful collection of wall decor and decorative pieces by fine artists and craftsmen. The latest cookbooks you'll find here, too. They host great events (like grilled cheese and wine tastings) plus appearances with artisans and chefs.

234 BERNAL CUTLERY

766 Valencia Street
Mission ⑤
+1 415 355 0773
bernalcutlery.com

A shop dedicated to knives, especially from Japan, France and vintage ones, too. The collection is impressive and the staff will happily guide you through blade and metal types, handles, care instructions and when sharpening might be required. They also host classes to help you hone your cutting and sharpening skills.

235 THE WOK SHOP

718 Grant Avenue
Chinatown ②
+1 415 989 3797
wokshop.com

For the ultimate stir-fry cooking, you need a wok and there's no better place to buy one than this shop in Chinatown. There are dozens of styles to choose from. The helpful staff offer great advice on caring for them. If you need other accessories like steamers and crocks, they stock those, too.

LE POINT

40 PLACES FOR FASHION & BEAUTY

———————

5 of the best
JEWELRY
shops

---

236 COLLEEN MAUER

1406 Valencia St B,
Suite B
Mission ⑤
+1 415 637 7762
colleenmauer
designs.com

Colleen and her team handcraft pieces that celebrate clean geometries and effortless angles. Everything is simple in design and perfect for the everyday. Many of her designs combine multiple metals (some oxidized) and her rings are wonderful for stacking. You can visit her small production studio and showroom in the Mission.

237 LOVE & LUXE

1169 Valencia Street
Mission ⑤
+1 415 648 7781
loveandluxesf.com

Owned and curated by artist Betsy Barron, this gallery and atelier showcases a unique collection of handcrafted jewelry and accessories by small studio artists, locally and worldwide. Many so distinct, edgy and wearable as art. You can opt to have a special piece custom designed by any of the artists, too.

238 METIER

546 Laguna Street
Hayes Valley ④
+1 415 590 2998
metiersf.com

A beautiful and thoughtful collection of modern and estate jewelry, accessories, pottery and other exquisite, one-of-a-kind finds. Whether new or vintage, each piece embodies a unique style and craftsmanship that will be cherished and worn over time. The shop is of a blue that just beckons you. It is a precious little space to visit.

239 NO.3

2354 Polk Street
Russian Hill ②
+1 415 525 4683
shopno3.com

A stunning mix of pieces from some of the most innovative jewelry designers out there. You'll find everyday adornments, a few statement ones, as well as some non-traditional bridal selections. They offer custom designs, too. Simple, modern, elegant yet edgy and plenty to choose from for stacking and layering.

240 SOKO

10 Arkansas Street
Potrero Hill ⑤
+1 628 300 0635
shopsoko.com

Here you'll find a collection of modern, ethical jewelry handcrafted by artisan entrepreneurs around the globe. And at accessible prices. Soko works with these artisans daily to develop their business and bring their talent to urban consumers. All pieces are simple and elegant, using mostly locally sourced and eco-friendly materials, like recycled brass.

5 shops for
SUSTAINABLE FASHION

---

241 AMOUR VERT

2110 Chestnut Street
Marina/Cow Hollow ①
+1 415 654 5385
amourvert.com

Sustainable, versatile, and thoughtfully designed women's clothing, and 97% of it is made in California and within miles of San Francisco. Local production also means less transportation and less carbon footprint. And with every purchase of a tee, they plant a tree in North America.

242 TONLÉ

55 Clement Street
Inner Richmond ⑦
+1 415 510 9405
tonle.com

Tonlé's mission is to reduce waste generated by larger factories and to change the way business is done in the fashion industry. They empower women in a developing nation and provide them with skills to create beautiful zero-waste clothing and accessories where every thread matters.

243 ROTHYS

2448 Fillmore Street
Pacific Heights ①
rothys.com/sf

This SF-based company designs and produces washable, woven flats and shoes made from recycled plastic. Since the beginning they've converted single-use plastics into something beautiful and useful. Millions of water bottles have been diverted from landfills and repurposed into shoes that are timeless and durable.

244 ALLBIRDS

57 Hotaling Place
Financial District ②
+1 415 469 1455
allbirds.com

The most comfortable casual footwear for men, women and children. Each pair is made from wool held to high standards of farming, land management and animal welfare, and shoelaces are made from plastic water bottles. And the shoes are washable.

245 REFORMATION

2360 Fillmore Street
Pacific Heights ①
thereformation.com

Most folks think hippie and hemp when they hear about eco and sustainable fashion. Reformation redefines that by designing modern, sexy, feminine silhouettes that celebrate and accentuate the female form, like floral-printed maxi dresses, blouses and fitted jumpsuits.

5

CASUAL WOMEN'S
shops

---

246 MARGARET O'LEARY

2400 Fillmore Street
Pacific Heights ①
+1 415 771 9982
margaretoleary.com

This local based company is known for easy, relaxed, California-chic knitwear. Their pieces are great for pairing with everyday essentials throughout the seasons. A great spot to invest in comfy sweaters and accessories you plan to wear for many years.

247 RELIQUARY

544 Hayes Street
Hayes Valley ④
+1 415 431 4000
reliquarysf.com

A folky collection of apparel, including cotton shirts, knits, linens and denim, as well as jewelry, accessories and handcrafted goods. And some vintage pieces added to the mix. The style can be described as Californian meets Southwestern.

248 CUYANA

291 Geary Street,
2nd Floor
Union Square ③
+1 415 445 3001
cuyana.com

Fewer, better things for your closet –
the concept of Cuyana. To find this gem,
you'll need to take the stairs or elevator
up to their showroom. It's simply
beautiful. Timeless pieces designed for
the modern woman using carefully
selected materials, precise silhouettes
and attention to detail.

249 EVERLANE

461 Valencia Street
Mission ⑤
everlane.com

Also founded in SF, Everlane provide great
modern basics and are best known for
being radically transparent about their
true costs, materials and process since
the beginning. All this information is
provided when you click on any product
online. Previously an online shop, this is
their flagship location to shop in person.

250 MODERN CITIZEN

2078 Union Street
Marina/Cow Hollow ①
+1 415 796 3807
moderncitizen.com

For those who love a capsule wardrobe
of continually stylish and versatile pieces.
All thoughtfully designed with great
silhouettes and approachable price points.
You'll always feel classic and current with
their collection.

5

CHIC WOMEN'S
shops

---

251 FREDA SALVADOR

2416 Fillmore Street
Pacific Heights ①
+1 415 872 9690
fredasalvador.com

A cult line of super-stylish, super-edgy and ever walkable footwear designed by two local Bay Area women. The design studio is nearby in Sausalito and all the shoes are handcrafted at a family factory in Spain. Casual and cool, you can wear these from day to night.

252 LE POINT

301 Valencia Street
Mission ⑤
+1 415 400 4275
shoplepoint.com

A beautiful, minimally designed, gallery-like space with an edited collection of garments from coveted brands, jewelry and a few accessories and home objects. Owner Pauline Montupet has impeccable taste and a sharp eye for detail having worked as a wardrobe stylist in her career.

253 ATELIER LAN JAENICKE

431 Jackson Street
Financial District ②
+1 415 766 4673
lanjaenicke.com

This may be the softest, most sumptuous shop in all of SF. By this, I mean luxurious textures of cashmere and silk. Lan's signature coats and jackets are coveted around the world, and this is her studio where she designs and showcases her collection.

254 HERO SHOP

982 Post Street
Tenderloin ③
+1 415 829 3129
heroshopsf.com

Former *Vogue* fashion editor and Bay Area native Emily Holt designed a unique space pairing global fashion ideas with local talent and offering a fun mix of ready-to-wear, jewelry, accessories, home and gift items. It's a treat to see style like this in the city. This shop brings it up a notch.

255 KIM + ONO

729 Grant Avenue
Chinatown ②
+1 415 989 8588
kimandono.com

A sweet boutique owned and operated by two sisters who've discovered a way to share the age-old tradition of the kimono with the modern world. They've designed beautiful botanical-inspired silk and charmeuse pieces that can be worn for intimate and special occasions, and casually for every day.

254 HERO SHOP

5
CASUAL MEN'S
shops

256 AB FITS

1519 Grant Avenue
North Beach/
Telegraph Hill ②
+1 415 982 5726
abfits.com

Quality clothing and proper fit. Howard, the owner, has an eye for these things and will help you find a style and fit, especially denim, that you'll feel good in. Try things on. And there's never any kind of upsell or pressure to buy. They also do hems and repairs, too.

257 WELCOME STRANGER

460 Gough Street
Hayes Valley ④
+1 415 864 2079
welcomestranger.com

A broad selection of comfortable, casual, everyday tees, chinos, jeans, outerwear, shoes and accessories. They have their own clothing line in the mix, too. It's a cool space with a cool vibe and service is neither pushy nor distant. Look around and stay awhile.

258 IRON & RESIN

7 Columbus Avenue
Financial District ②
+1 415 624 3288
ironandresin.com

Founded by several friends is this small, handbuilt collection of goods, including graphic tees, bottoms, outerwear, headwear and other accessories. The focus is on owning fewer, quality things that last a long time. If any of their goods fail on you, they will happily repair or replace it.

259 MARINE LAYER

1572 California St
Nob Hill ②
+1 415 970 5785
marinelayer.com

This local company designs some of the softest T-shirts out there – just like the old worn favorites you don't want to get rid of. The collection has expanded to include other garments, outerwear and accessories for men, women and children. And this location serves as their workshop space.

260 HANDSOME OXFORD

646 Hyde Street
Tenderloin ③
+1 510 673 0776

These folks offer old-school American-made clothing and accessories, including vintage sports apparel, 70s Levi's, wool blankets, camping gear and even stuff for tots. It's geared mostly for men. The owners drive up along the West Coast searching for cool goods to introduce in the shop.

5

CHIC and CUSTOM
MEN'S shops

261 CABLE CAR CLOTHIERS

110 Sutter Street,
Suite 108
Financial District ②
+1 415 397 4740
cablecarclothiers.com

This place is for all the dapper gentlemen out there. It is a classic 1930s style barbershop plus a haberdashery of fine suits, sport coats, hats, footwear, travel bags and other men's accessories. Get fitted for a custom jacket, don a Fedora or see Nicky the Barber for a proper shave and trim.

262 SELF EDGE

714 Valencia Street
Mission ⑤
+1 415 558 0658
selfedge.com

Japanese and other premium denim: it's here and it's not cheap. But investing in a good pair can last you for years to come. For those meticulous about denim and value its quality, they have a great staff to help you select a pair along with other garments and accessories. They do repairs, too.

263 TAILORS' KEEP

618 Washington St
Financial District ②
+1 415 944 2615
tailorskeep.com

For made-to-measure bespoke suits and clothing, trust these guys to help you look your best. They are great about educating on fabrics, linings, buttons and take their time measuring you to ensure the perfect fit. Turnaround time is generally seven weeks so plan your visit accordingly.

264 TAYLOR STITCH

383 Valencia Street
Mission ⑤
+1 415 621 2231
taylorstitch.com

Classic, well constructed, super quality, design-your-own and locally made in the U.S. menswear and accessories. Plus some ready-to-wear from other makers, too. A cool place to peruse and attentive service without all the pretense.

265 WINGTIP

550 Montgomery St
Financial District ②
+1 415 765 0993
wingtip.club

Formerly a bank and now a national historic landmark, Wingtip is both a store and modern gentlemen's club. On the bottom levels are professional and casual clothing, accessories, wines and spirits, cigars, a barbershop and home furnishings. The members-only club with a bar, entertainment lounges, parlors and a wine cellar occupy the penthouse floors.

264 TAYLOR STITCH

5 of the coolest
BARBER
shops

---

266 FELLOW BARBER

973 Market Street
SoMa ③
+1 415 344 0443
fellowbarber.com

There are two locations in the city and this is the newer one. It's a cool, relaxed place for men to get a hair or beard trim. Appointments with a Barber or Senior Barber can be made in advance online and you can play a game of pool while you wait. They've also developed their own products line.

267 SAVIOURS SALON

3382 18th Street
Mission ⑤
+1 415 962 7881
saviourssalon.com

A quaint and quirky salon for great cuts and color. Truly eclectic interior and a terrific vinyl collection which make getting your hair done there fun. Enjoy a glass of whiskey while you're at it. Be sure you use the loo even if you don't have to. It's very 60s surf-glam in there.

268 VEER & WANDER

6 Brady Street
SoMa ③
+1 415 864 3012
veerandwander.com

An ultra-chic, modern-day apothecary and salon. Get your hair done, then pop into the adjoining space to peruse the most unique brands and selections of hair products, fragrances, skincare, makeup and accessories gathered from around the world. The vibe is very dark, moody and sexy.

269 **PEOPLES BARBER**

1259 Polk Street
Nob Hill ③
+1 415 292 4099
peoplesbarber.com

For the gentleman, Peoples has two locations in the city. They are a full-service, luxury barber offering haircuts, shaves and beard trims at reasonable prices. Beer and bourbon are also offered with your treatment. It's best to make an appointment as they can only accommodate so many walk-ins.

270 **POPULATION**

537 Divisadero Street
NoPa ④
+1 415 440 7677
populationsalon.com

Population has two locations. This one in the NoPa area and the other in the Mission. Each offers cut and color and complimentary tea, wine, beer and water with your service. Appointments should be made in advance. The spaces are styled with Victorian furnishings and antique lighting, and this one's like an old piano bar.

268 **VEER & WANDER**

5 places to
GET PAMPERED

---

271 INTERNATIONAL ORANGE

2044 Fillmore Street,
2nd Floor
Pacific Heights ①
+1 415 563 5000
international
orange.com

A little oasis in the city for spectacular facials and massages. It is minimally designed and very intimate. No large groups convening and chatting here. Relax in the lounge or the zen patio and enjoy bites of dark chocolate and dried apricots along with a hot cup of tea.

272 KABUKI SPRINGS & SPA

1750 Geary Blvd
Japantown ④
+1 415 922 6000
kabukisprings.com

Massages, facials and other spa treatments accompanied by a Japanese-style bathing experience, which includes a seated wash area, a hot pool, cold plunge, dry sauna and steam room. Certain days are dedicated to either men or women only. Tuesdays are co-ed. Book the bath experience only or add it to a service.

273 ONSEN

466 Eddy Street
Tenderloin ③
+1 415 441 4987
onsensf.com

Another intimate Japanese bath house with a small offering of treatments (massage and acupuncture), as well as evening restaurant with a seasonal menu. There is a communal tub, sauna, steam room and showers. Wednesday are men only and Thursdays are for women.

274 SENSPA

1161 Gorgas Avenue
Presidio ①
+1 415 441 1777
senspa.com

Tucked in the Presidio is this hidden oasis for massage therapy, facials and other wellness treatments, with several relaxing rooms to settle into before and after your appointment. It's located in one of the most quiet parts of SF, so it's a nice escape from the bustle of the city.

275 PEARL SPA & SAUNA

1654 Post Street
Japantown ④
+1 415 580 7142
pearlspasf.com

Book an oil massage and scrub off layers of dead skin cells at this Korean spa. With those treatments, you get unlimited use of the facilities (sauna, hot and cold tubs, shower, salt room, clay room) and lounge. The facility is nice and clean and be sure to bring some cash for tipping.

273 ONSEN

JAPANESE TEA GARDEN

65 PLACES
TO DISCOVER SF

———

5 unique
HISTORIC HOMES
to visit

---

276 HAAS-LILIENTHAL HOUSE

2007 Franklin Street
Pacific Heights ⓘ
+1 415 441 3000
sfheritage.org/
haas-lilienthal-house

If you're wondering what life was like in a grand Victorian for a better than average family at the turn of the 19th century, visit this home. It's filled with original furnishings, clothing and even a giant antique train set. You can sign up for a tour of the house or a walking one of the neighborhood.

277 MCELROY OCTAGON HOUSE

2645 Gough Street
Marina/Cow Hollow ⓘ
+1 415 441 7512
nscda-ca.org/
octagon-house

During the 19th century some believed a house of this shape was a more efficient use of space, energy and cost than a typical square kind. That was short lived and this is one of three remaining octagon homes in the city. A historic landmark, it is now a museum of period arts, craft and furniture.

278 SPRECKELS MANSION

2080 Washington St
Pacific Heights ⓘ

This impressive chateau was built for sugar tycoon Adolph Spreckels and his wife, Alma. A love story of a rich, older man and a poor, younger woman who lived in the finest home in the city. It sits on an entire half block in the city and has its own crooked road.

279 ABNER PHELPS HOUSE

1111 Oak Street
Haight-Ashbury ④

The oldest house in SF, it was constructed around 1850 for Abner Phelps, a colonel in the Mexican-American War and lawyer in the city. Where it was built before it was assembled in SF remains a mystery. The house is pushed much further back from its neighbors enabling Abner to build stores on nearby Divisadero Street.

280 TOBIN HOUSE

1969 California St
Pacific Heights ①

What appears as a half completed home was meant to be two. Michael De Young (founder of the *San Francisco Chronicle*) intended for his daughters to occupy two mirroring houses. One was happy to live there; the other was not. The second house was never built, which explains the abruptly ending archway.

278 SPRECKELS MANSION

5 places as
SEEN IN THE MOVIES

---

281 MOUNT DAVIDSON CROSS
DIRTY HARRY (1971)
39 Dalewood Way
(start of trailhead)
Sherwood Forest ⑥
sfrecpark.org/
destination/
mt-davidson-park

This is where Clint Eastwood's famous scene from the 1971 classic, *Dirty Harry*, was filmed. Wind your way through the park and head to the white cross at the summit where Harry Callahan brings the ransom money and ultimately meets the psychotic Scorpio. You can 'put your nose right up to the cement', as Clint did.

282 ALLEYWAY
MALTESE FALCON (1941)
Burritt and Bush St
Union Square ③

Burritt Street marks the place where the character Miles Archer, partner of Sam Spade (played by Humphrey Bogart) was killed by Brigid O'Shaughnessy. There is even a plaque in this alley to commemorate it. To find this spot, head up the stairs to reach the top of the tunnel and walk a half block.

282 ALLEYWAY IN *THE MALTESE FALCON*

285 LEGION OF HONOR IN *VERTIGO*

283 MRS. DOUBTFIRE'S HOUSE
MRS. DOUBTFIRE (1993)

**2640 Steiner Street
Pacific Heights ①**

This iconic Victorian is the family home of Miranda Hillard (played by Sally Field) where ex-husband Daniel Hillard (played by Robin Williams) disguises as a housekeeper, Mrs. Doubtfire, in order to spend more time with his children. Many scenes were filmed at this location and fans of the beloved late actor flock here to pay their tributes.

284 CITY HALL
RAIDERS OF THE LOST ARK (1981)

**1 Dr Carlton
B Goodlett Place
Civic Center ③
+1 415 554 4000
*sfgov.org/cityhall***

Filming took place in many parts of the world, but the final scene, set in Washington D.C., was actually filmed on the grand steps of San Francisco's City Hall. It is open to the public during business hours and you can descend the staircase as Indy and Marion (portrayed by Harrison Ford and Karen Allen) did.

285 LEGION OF HONOR
VERTIGO (1958)
AT: LINCOLN PARK

**100 34th Avenue
Sea Cliff ⑦
+1 415 750 3600
*legionofhonor.
famsf.org***

The infamous *Portrait of Carlotta* scene in Alfred Hitchcock's SF-based thriller. Head to the museum's Gallery 6 to see where Scotty (James Stewart) observes Madeleine (Kim Novak) on a bench staring at a painting of a woman who bears a striking resemblance to her. The exterior of the museum was also featured in the film.

5 of the city's
STEEPEST HILLS

In 2009 local datasmith Stephen Von Worley set out to find SF's steepest paved public streets. He achieved this by combining national elevation data with an OpenStreetMap grid along with some urban exploring. His final list included all paved roads he could find, regardless of length. Some turned out to be elevated driveways or sidewalk-only streets where cars weren't allowed.

Using Von Worley's data as a starting point, the *Priceonomics* team ventured on their own hill hunting and expanded on his findings. Using an inclinometer to measure grade, they rode their bicycle on these hills over three days. They found the five hills listed here to be the steepest in the city.

Bottom line: San Francisco has many hills, so know how to maneuver your vehicle and wear comfortable shoes.

Source:
Priceonomics; data via Data Pointed, field research (bike rides through the city)

286 BRADFORD ST ABOVE TOMPKINS AVE

HILL GRADE: 41%

Bernal Heights ⑤

287 BRODERICK ST BETWEEN BROADWAY AND VALLEJO ST

HILL GRADE: 38%

Pacific Heights ①

288 ROMOLO PLACE BETWEEN VALLEJO AND FRESNO ST

HILL GRADE: 38%

North Beach/
Telegraph Hill ②

289 PRENTISS ST BETWEEN CHAPMAN ST AND POWHATTAN AVE

HILL GRADE: 37%

Bernal Heights ⑤

290 NEVADA ST ABOVE CHAPMAN ST

HILL GRADE: 35%

Bernal Heights ⑤

5

HILLS WORTH CLIMBING
for the view

---

291 TELEGRAPH HILL

1 Telegraph Hill Blvd
North Beach/
Telegraph Hill ②
*sfrecpark.org/
destination/
telegraph-hill-pioneer-
park/coit-tower*

You'll find so much more than just the views from up here. Exquisite homes, garden-filled stairwells and squawking wild green parrots await. For even better views, take the elevator up to the observation deck of Coit Tower and enjoy the breathtaking, panoramic landscapes, especially of the North and East Bays.

292 BERNAL HILL

Bernal Heights Blvd
Bernal Heights ⑤
*sfrecpark.org/
destination/
bernal-heights-park*

Head to the top for clear, 360-degree panoramic views of the city, including downtown, the Golden Gate Bridge, the peninsula and the East Bay. You'll also find a rope swing and a painted rock that continuously gets a colorful and humorous makeover. The latter is located on the north side of the hill.

293 BILLY GOAT HILL

30th and Castro St
Noe Valley ⑤
sfrecpark.org/
destination/
billy-goat-hill

Enjoy a pretty vista of the city from up here, and cross your fingers there's a rope swing. It feels as if you're swinging into an abyss. Often it gets cut down, then some kind person will set up another. Even without it, it's a nice climb and a perfect spot to perch down for a bit.

294 TANK HILL

Clarendon Ave and
Twin Peaks Blvd
Clarendon Heights ⑥
+1 415 753 7265
sfrecpark.org/
destination/tank-hill-
natural-areas

Its name comes from a prominent tank that once occupied the hill and stored drinking water that was pumped nearby. At 200 meters high, this centrally located mini park is still one of the lesser-known hills and offers outstanding views of the city and beyond. It is also home to dozens of native plant species.

295 TWIN PEAKS

501 Twin Peaks Blvd
Twin Peaks ⑥
+1 415 831 2700
sfrecpark.org/
destination/twin-peaks

At 280 meters high, these two adjacent peaks are the busiest of San Francisco hills. Expect many pedestrians, cars and busses to be convened at top for postcard views of the city, but the climb is worth it. It is also located at the geographical center of SF and provides a perfect lookout in all directions.

5 of the lushest
URBAN GARDENS
to wander

---

296 FILBERT AND GREENWICH STREET STEPS

START AT: COIT TOWER
1 Telegraph Hill Blvd
North Beach/
Telegraph Hill ②

From Coit Tower venture down the lush wooden walkway and stroll past some of the city's oldest Victorian-era cottages and private gardens. And you might also spot the famous wild green parrots that come here to perch, too. Once a trash-filled path back in 1949, it is now one of San Francisco's most gorgeous garden oases.

297 FLORA GRUBB GARDENS

1634 Jerrold Avenue
Bayview/
Hunters Point ⑤
+1 415 626 7256
floragrubb.com

Here you'll find an amazing selection of plants and succulent arrangements, some displayed in unique ways for fun and inspiration, like in a sink or the interior of a vehicle. Grab a cup of coffee from the cafe and soak up the sun and beautiful surroundings from the garden's many seating areas.

298 **CONSERVATORY OF FLOWERS**

300 **SF BOTANICAL GARDEN**

298 CONSERVATORY OF FLOWERS

100 John F. Kennedy Drive
Golden Gate Park ⑥
+1 415 831 2090
conservatoryof flowers.org

A stunning Victorian greenhouse that happens to be the oldest public wood-and-glass conservatory in North America. Experience different microclimates as you go room-to-room discovering the range of aquatic, tropical and potted plants on display. There's even a Corpse Flower. Many fascinating events and exhibits are held throughout the year, so check the calendar.

299 JAPANESE TEA GARDEN

75 Hagiwara Tea Garden Drive
Golden Gate Park ⑥
+1 415 752 1171
japanesetea gardensf.com

This is the oldest public Japanese garden in the U.S. and visitors come from all parts of the world to experience its beauty and tranquility. Walk over an arched drum bridge, take the stone paths, and visit the zen garden, pagodas and teahouse. In March and April the cherry blossoms bloom.

300 SAN FRANCISCO BOTANICAL GARDEN

9th Avenue and Lincoln Way
Golden Gate Park ⑥
+1 415 661 1316
sfbotanicalgarden.org

One of the most peaceful places you'll find in the city, it is 55 acres of open space showcasing over 8000 species of plants from around the world. Hide under a grove of mighty California redwood trees, walk through a cactus jungle and explore the collections in the Andean Cloud Forest.

5 great

P O P O S (Privately Owned Public Open Spaces) to unwind

—————

301 **1 KEARNY ROOFTOP**
ENTRANCE: 23 GEARY BLVD
Financial District ③
+1 415 788 1133

To reach the terrace look for the 'Public Open Space' sign on the Geary Street side of the building. You'll need to sign in and provide identification to gain access. Once cleared, enjoy the city views and an impressive backdrop of a decorative green roof from the tower next door.

302 **LINKEDIN PLAZA**
222 Second Street
SoMa ③

You don't have to be an employee to enter the lobby area of this major tech hub. The massive, enclosed space has floor-to-ceiling windows and doors, plenty of natural light, tables and chairs, stadium seating and also boasts a cafe, restrooms and free Wi-Fi.

303 **APPLE UNION SQUARE – THE PLAZA**
300 Post Street
Union Square ③
+1 415 486 4800
*apple.com/retail/
unionsquare*

Of course you'll need free Wi-Fi and open space to enjoy your shiny new Apple devices. The Plaza is located outside the store and offers both those plus art, including a famous 1969 San Francisco fountain by sculptor Ruth Asawa and a rainbow 'LOVE' sculpture by local artist Laura Kimpton.

304 CITIGROUP CENTER ATRIUM

1 Sansome Street
Financial District ②
+1 415 541 8580

Formerly the site of the ornate Anglo and London Paris National Bank, the atrium features stunning white marble walls and floors plus a glass ceiling. One of the 90 Star Maiden statues from the city's legendary 1915 Panama-Pacific Exposition is also displayed here. Today it's a peaceful spot to bring your lunch.

305 TRANSAMERICA REDWOOD PARK

600 Montgomery St
Financial District ②
pyramidcenter.com

At the foot of the city's iconic pyramid building is this serene grove shaded by towering redwood trees, sculptures and a fountain filled with jumping frog sculptures – a tribute to author Mark Twain who used to write in the park. It's a popular spot to unwind as there are plenty of tables and seating.

301 **1 KEARNY ROOFTOP**

5

THINGS THAT ARE GOLD
(the Golden Gate Bridge is not)

---

306 THE GARDEN COURT
AT: PALACE HOTEL
2 New Montgomery
Street
SoMa ③
+1 415 546 5089
*sfpalace.com/
garden-court*

Located within San Francisco's most elegant landmark hotel, The Garden Court dining room glimmers in gold with its chandeliers, rich features and warm light radiating through its glass ceilings. It's a gorgeous setting to enjoy afternoon high tea service or to settle down for evening drinks, bites and entertainment.

307 THE GOLDEN FIRE HYDRANT
Church and 20th St
Dolores Heights ⑤

This little fire hydrant was a major hero during the 1906 earthquake and fire. While other city hydrants failed, this one remained functional and was key to the survival of the neighborhood. Every April 18 (the anniversary of the devastation), it's given a fresh coat of gold paint and is honored by the city's grateful citizens.

308 THE PACIFIC BELL BUILDING LOBBY
140 New
Montgomery Street
SoMa ③

Step through the glass doors and enter the lobby of this gorgeous art deco building. Once inside look all around, as everything from the ceilings to the elevators and window frames are trimmed in gold. It's exquisite.

309 LOTTA'S FOUNTAIN

Kearny and Market St
Financial District ③

This golden fountain was commissioned by entertainer and philanthropist Lotta Crabtree in 1875. Crabtree started her career in SF during the Gold Rush Days, dancing with miners who would throw gold at her feet. She then used much of it to buy the city she loved this fountain. It is the oldest monument surviving the city's many earthquakes and fires.

310 SAMUEL'S CLOCK
IN FRONT OF:

856 Market Street
Union Square ③

This city landmark was installed in 1915 to celebrate the opening of the Panama-Pacific International Exposition. Albert Samuels immigrated from Austria to the city in 1893. He became a watchmaker, opening his shop at 895 Market Street in 1909. When he moved the business to 856 Market Street in 1943, the clock moved with him where it remains to this day.

306 THE GARDEN COURT

5 must-see spots in
CHINATOWN

---

311 ALLEYS OF CHINATOWN
Ross, Waverly, Duncombe, Beckett, Cooper, Wentworth and St. Louis Alleys
Chinatown ②

There are over 40 alleys in this small section of the city and the ones listed here are the more notable ones. In the 1800s and early 1900s these were the sites of former gambling halls, brothels, opium dens and other daily activities, like fish markets and barbershops. Look up each alley's unique history as you encounter them.

312 GOLDEN GATE FORTUNE COOKIE FACTORY
56 Ross Alley
Chinatown ②
+1 415 781 3956

Along this alley you'll get a whiff of sweetness coming from this tiny factory, which has been making fortune cookies for SF and around the world since 1962. A few dollars gets you a bag full and another 50 cents allows you to get up close and take pictures of the process. And they give out free samples, too.

313 TIN HOW (TIEN HAU) TEMPLE
125 Waverly Place
Chinatown ②
+1 415 986 2520

Find the doorway along this alley and be prepared to climb several flights of stairs. And take note, photos are not allowed. Once inside you'll see it's a small, decorative and sacred space for prayer and worship. For visitors, simply enjoy the peace and silence.

314 STREET OF PAINTED BALCONIES

Waverly Place (betw Washington and Sacramento Street)
Chinatown ②

This area is comprised of two blocks and today is known as the 'Street of Painted Balconies' for its colorful and ornate buildings. Of all the Chinatown alleys, it's the most picturesque. On street level are restaurants and storefronts, and above are family associations and temples.

315 PORTSMOUTH SQUARE

Kearny Street (between Clay and Washington)
Chinatown ②

Considered the heart of Chinatown, this park hosted many historical events, including the first raising of the American flag within the city in 1846, the opening of the first public school in California in 1847, and this is also the place where the discovery of gold was first announced in 1848. There are historical markers and statues throughout the park.

314 STREET OF PAINTED BALCONIES

5 places to discover
THE SUMMER OF LOVE

316 (FORMERLY) THE AVALON BALLROOM

1244 Sutter Street
Nob Hill ③

This venue lasted only from 1966 to 1969, but this is where Janis Joplin and Big Brother and the Holding Company performed for those few years. She left Texas to join The Band in SF and their music took off to mainstream. The building is now owned by an ad agency, but its history and Janis' spirit live on.

317 THE FILLMORE

1805 Geary Blvd
Fillmore ④
+1 415 346 6000
thefillmore.com

This legendary venue opened in 1912, but the late 1960s was the real pinnacle of creative music, especially psychedelic rock, with bands like The Grateful Dead and Jefferson Airplane. Enter and head up the stairs to find photos and posters of every legend that's ever played there. Imagine if those walls could talk.

318 GRATEFUL DEAD HOUSE

710 Ashbury Street
Haight-Ashbury ⑥

This purple Victorian was once occupied by Jerry Garcia and members of The Band during the 1960s. You can't go inside, but you can pose for photos outside the front gate and maybe see some Deadhead art on the sidewalk. Be respectful, as there are occupants now living in the house.

319 HAIGHT-ASHBURY

START AT:
Haight and
Stanyan Street
Haight-Ashbury ⑥

Walk down Haight Street between Stanyan and Masonic and you'll see and feel the hippie power is still alive. Peruse the vibrant street art, shop for paraphernalia and frocks, watch street performers and relax in the park. And pop into Amoeba to browse music from that Summer of Love.

320 HIPPIE HILL

AT: GOLDEN GATE PARK
Stanyan Street
and Kezar Drive
Golden Gate Park ⑥

The infamous meadow and hill where the artists, musicians and flower children gathered in the 1960s. Today you'll still see the happy folk convening, drumming in circles, and let me just say it … getting high. There is also a tree that bears Janis Joplin's name. You'll find this spot on the eastern end of Golden Gate Park.

5 spots of
THE BEAT GENERATION

---

321 THE BEAT MUSEUM

540 Broadway
North Beach/
Telegraph Hill ②
+1 415 399 9626
kerouac.com

Keeping the spirit of the Beat Generation alive, the museum houses an extensive collection of original works, including manuscripts, first editions, letters, art and personal effects of these non-conformists. You'll even find the Hudson vehicle Jack Kerouac and Neal Cassady drove around in.

322 CAFFE TRIESTE

601 Vallejo Street
North Beach/
Telegraph Hill ②
+1 415 392 6739
coffee.caffetrieste.com/
nbeach

Not only is this the first espresso coffee house established on the West Coast (1956), it was also a well-known respite for the bohemian writers, poets and artists of that time. There are old photos of them lining the walls. A new generation of free-thinkers and long time locals continue to frequent this cafe.

323 NEAL AND CAROLYN CASSADY'S HOME

29 Russell Street
Russian Hill ②

This is where Neal and Carolyn Cassady lived in the 1950s and where Jack Kerouac would often visit and stay. Kerouac occupied the attic in early 1952 while writing *Visions of Cody,* and the legendary character of Dean Moriarty in his classic *On The Road* was closely based on his good pal Neal.

324 JACK KEROUAC ALLEY / CITY LIGHTS BOOKSTORE

261 Columbus Ave
Chinatown ②
+1 415 362 8193
citylights.com

These two wouldn't exist without poet and activist Lawrence Ferlinghetti. As founder of the bookstore and its publishing wing, he published the work of many Beat Generation writers. The alley alongside was used for garbage dumping and he proposed a new pedestrian walkway to the city. The new alley features colorful murals and quotes from writers, including Jack Kerouac.

325 VESUVIO CAFE

255 Columbus Ave
Chinatown ②
+1 415 362 3370
vesuvio.com

This two-level saloon opened in 1948 and was regularly frequented by celebrities of the Beat Generation. It was a beloved spot to meet, enjoy drinks and write. Their spirit is kept alive with era posters and photos of them filling the space. The bar continues to attract a bohemian crowd to this day.

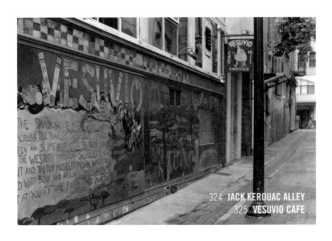

324 JACK KEROUAC ALLEY
325 VESUVIO CAFE

5 unique discoveries in
GOLDEN GATE PARK

326 ALVORD LAKE BRIDGE

Enter the park from
Stanyan and Haight St
Golden Gate Park ⑥

Built in 1889, this overlooked engineering marvel was designed by Ernest Ransome, innovator of reinforced concrete strengthened with steel bars. A few years after the bridge, Ransome left SF, as builders were indifferent to his method. Ironically, during the 1906 earthquake, this bridge and the few other reinforced concrete structures survived in great shape.

327 BUFFALO PADDOCK

John F. Kennedy
Drive and Chain of
Lakes Drive East
Golden Gate Park ⑥
*goldengatepark.com/
buffalo-paddock.html*

They're actually bison and these fine creatures have been arriving to the city since 1890. The small population of them has changed over the years, but they're kept as part of a successful captive breeding program to increase their population in North America. An odd sight to see, but a remarkable one, too.

328 DUTCH AND MURPHY WINDMILLS

John F. Kennedy Dr
near Great Hwy
Golden Gate Park ⑥
+1 415 263 0991
goldengatepark.com/
windmills.html

In the late 1800s the park rested on sand dunes and required assistance with irrigation. These windmills were built to pump water for that purpose. Electric pumps replaced the need for windmills in 1913, and these fell into disrepair over the decades. Both were restored end of the 20th century and tulips bloom nearby in February and March.

329 FAERY (FAIRY) DOOR

Look up clues and
directions online
Golden Gate Park ⑥

To find this tiny door, start at the Japanese Tea Garden and find clues and directions from your device. It was designed by artist Tony Powell and his son, and those who find it will often leave messages, questions and trinkets for the fairies. The artist maintains a website where he occasionally responds on behalf of the fairies.

330 RAINBOW FALLS AND PRAYER BOOK CROSS

John F. Kennedy Dr
near Park Presidio
Boulevard
Golden Gate Park ⑥
goldengatepark.com/
the-waterfalls-of-
golden-gate-park.html

One of two artificial waterfalls in the park, this one got its name from the colored lights that once illuminated it. Today it is a unique site to visit and if you take the trail to the top, you will encounter the park's tallest structure: a massive, 20-meter-high Celtic cross dating back to 1894.

5 great attractions in
THE PRESIDIO

---

331 ANDY GOLDSWORTHY SCULPTURES

Various locations
Presidio ⓘ

Woodline. Spire. Fallen Tree. Earth Wall.
All masterpieces by one of the world's
most renowned artists hidden within
the Presidio. Andy constructs sculptures
using nature's gifts, knowing one day
they'll crumble or fade into the earth,
so enjoy them while they're still around.
To see all four works, use a map to
navigate this 5-km loop.

332 FORT POINT

Long Avenue and
Marine Drive
Presidio ⓘ
+1 415 504 2334
nps.gov/fopo/index.htm

This fort was built in the 1850s during
the Gold Rush to protect the Bay against
foreign attacks, however it never saw
battle. Today it's a National Historic
Site and outdoor museum. The best
part, really, is its position on the water
right below the Golden Gate Bridge.
It's a remarkable view.

33 | ANDY GOLDSWORTHY SCULPTURES

333 LUCASARTS

1110 Gorgas Avenue
Presidio ⓘ
lucasfilm.com
lucasarts.com

Here lies the headquarters where development of the *Star Wars* and *Indiana Jones* franchise takes place, as well as visual effects for blockbusters like *Harry Potter*. Visitors can stop by the main lobby on weekdays to see the life-size Darth Vader and other film props. The Yoda fountain can be seen anytime outside the entrance.

334 PALACE OF FINE ARTS

3301 Lyon Street
Presidio ⓘ
+1 415 563 6504
palaceoffinearts.org

Imagine this entire waterfront filled with the most ornamental buildings, courtyards, gardens, fountains and a tower glistening with jewels. That was SF during the 1915 Panama-Pacific Exposition and this palace is the last to remain in the area. It's been rebuilt since, and its presence by the pond makes it the most spectacular sight in the city.

335 PRESIDIO OFFICERS' CLUB

50 Moraga Avenue
Presidio ⓘ
+1 415 561 5300
presidio.gov/officers-club

This museum and cultural center provides a glimpse into the Presidio's past and present through galleries and exhibitions. It also offers free live music, talks and weekend crafts for kids. The story of the Presidio goes back as far as 10.000 years ago. Andy Goldsworthy's *Earth Wall* (previously mentioned) can be found here.

5

OLD RUINS

worth discovering

---

336 FORT MILEY BATTERIES TO LANDS END OCTAGON HOUSE
START AT:
4150 Clement Street
Sea Cliff ⑦
+1 415 561 4700
*nps.gov/nr/travel/
wwiibayarea/mil.htm*

Built in 1899, this military stronghold was built to protect the city from attack through WWII. A cemetery dating back to the Gold Rush had to be cleared first. What remains are the empty gun batteries and an octagon house which kept eye on incoming ships at the Golden Gate. All these are well hidden by trees.

337 PORTALS OF THE PAST
AT: LLOYD LAKE
John F. Kennedy
Drive near
Transverse Drive
Golden Gate Park ⑥
*sfrecpark.org/
destination/golden-
gate-park/portals-of-
the-past*

These pillars once graced the entrance of railroad tycoon Alban Towne's Nob Hill mansion. The home and much of SF was destroyed in the 1906 devastation, and photographer Arnold Genthe caught an iconic image of the city's destruction framed between these columns. The portals were then placed on the lake as a symbol of perseverance for the city.

338 **SUTRO BATHS**

337 **PORTALS OF THE PAST**

338 SUTRO BATHS

1004 Point Lobos Ave
Sea Cliff ⑦
+1 415 426 5240
nps.gov/goga

Once the world's largest indoor swimming complex with glass ceilings, slides, swings, trampolines and plenty of amusement. Though the oceanside baths were popular, it wasn't profitable and was expensive to maintain. It closed in 1965 and what remains today are concrete and steel ruins. A great area to explore at sunset.

339 SUTRO HEIGHTS PARK RUINS

846 Point Lobos Ave
Sea Cliff ⑦
nps.gov/goga

This was the estate of millionaire and former mayor Adolph Sutro. It included a public garden with an observatory, conservatory, parapet and hundreds of statues. The Sutros lived here until 1938, when Adolph's daughter Emma died and the land was donated to the city. All is gone, but the parapet remains and offers perfect views of the ocean.

340 WRECK OF THE KING PHILIP

Ocean Beach near
Noriega Street
Outer Sunset ⑥

The King Philip clipper ship was built in 1856 and wrecked here in 1878. It was beyond repair and auctioned for its scrap. Its masts, sails and fittings were stripped, but sightings of its bow and stern will occur every few years during very low tides. If you time your visit accordingly, you might get a lucky glimpse.

JUNGLE HOUSE

55 PLACES
FOR ART & CULTURE

———

5

MUSEUMS *to visit*
AFTER DARK

---

341 ALCATRAZ NIGHT TOUR

Alcatraz Island
+1 415 981 7625
alcatrazcruises.com

Check out the city's most famous spot, but at night with less of a crowd and a view of the city and sunset. It's an eerie experience wandering the halls and cells of a penitentiary that once housed many of the most notorious criminals. Dress in layers. It's spooky and chilly.

342 EXPLORATORIUM AFTER DARK

Pier 15
Embarcadero ②
+1 415 528 4444
exploratorium.edu

Every Thursday night at 6 pm, grab some friends and play with over 650 interactive exhibits at this art and science museum. Find your way through a pitch black dome and play with a giant kaleidoscope. There's music, guest speakers and booze to enjoy, too. 21 and over.

343 THURSDAY NIGHTS AT ASIAN ART MUSEUM

200 Larkin Street
Civic Center ③
+1 415 581 3500
asianart.org

Explore the museum Thursday evenings from 5 to 9 pm and enjoy music, beverages and demonstrations with guest artists, performers, chefs and speakers. Each evening offers a unique experience, so it's good to check the line-up on the website to find programs that interest you.

344 THURSDAY NIGHTS AT SFMOMA

151 3rd Street
SoMa ③
+1 415 357 4000
sfmoma.org

This contemporary and modern art museum is open until 9 pm Thursday evenings. An opportunity for those who want to visit their favorite exhibit or pieces after work, and those who'd enjoy a night stroll through the galleries. Private guided tours are available and the restaurant stays open.

345 NIGHTLIFE AT CALIFORNIA ACADEMY OF SCIENCES

55 Music
Concourse Drive
Golden Gate Park ⑥
+1 415 379 8000
calacademy.org/
nightlife

Explore all the natural exhibits – from the stars above to the bottom of the sea – with music, food and cocktails every Thursday evening from 6 to 10 pm. Each event is focused on a theme (*Star Wars* and the galactic universe, for example), so check the calendar first. For ages 21 and over.

5
LOCAL ART GALLERIES
worth checking out

---

346 3 FISH STUDIOS
4541 Irving Street
Outer Sunset ⑥
+1 415 242 3474
3fishstudios.com

Eric Rewitzer and Annie Galvin are printmakers and painters, husband and wife, and at their workshop they create colorful and whimsy pieces depictive of the culture and landscape around the state and of the fun things swirling in their imagination. Their most recognized work is the 'I Love You California' bear.

347 CREATIVITY EXPLORED
3245 16th Street
Mission ⑤
+1 415 863 2108
creativityexplored.org

This organization exists to support those with developmental disabilities in their journey to become working artists. Through sales of their artwork, they provide these individuals the opportunity to earn income and pursue a livelihood as such. Visit the gallery to see some of their great work on display.

348 MINNESOTA STREET PROJECT
1275 Minnesota St
Potrero Hill ⑤
+1 415 243 0825
minnesotastreet project.com

In Potrero are three warehouses occupied by artists, galleries and related nonprofits in the contemporary art community. The galleries of two warehouses always have unique exhibits and they are free and open to the public to visit. Check hours online and plan to stay a few hours.

349 LOST ART SALON

**245 South Van Ness
Avenue, Suite 303
Mission** ⑤
+1 415 861 1530
lostartsalon.com

A truly unique and welcoming art browsing and buying experience. It's an industrial loft that's more Parisian-style apartment with paintings, drawings, prints, photographs, sculptures and ceramics filling every wall and surface – most by late 19th- and 20th-century artists. There are thousands of works to browse and admire from this very home-like gallery.

350 THE WORKSHOP RESIDENCE

**797 22nd Street
Dogpatch** ⑤
+1 415 285 2050
workshopresidence.com

This open studio and retail space features unique, yet functional objects for the everyday by local and visiting artists and designers, some taking residency in the space. Artists explore new materials and fabrication methods into their design.

348 MINNESOTA STREET PROJECT

5

ART INSTALLATIONS
that illuminate SF

---

351 THE BAY LIGHTS
Bay Bridge
Embarcadero ②
thebaylights.org

Designed by Leo Villareal, the western span of the bridge is now illuminated with 25.000 white LED lights that twinkle every evening from dusk to dawn. Originally planned as a two-year installation, it is now a permanent one. Stroll along the Embarcadero to witness this shimmering light show.

352 LANGUAGE OF THE BIRDS
Broadway St and Columbus Ave
Chinatown ②
metaphorm.org/works/language-of-the-birds

Look up to see this hanging installation (designed by Brian Goggin and Dorka Keehn) which features a flock of 23 illuminated books that mimic birds in flight. The pages and bindings acting as wings. Beneath the flock are words in English, Italian and Chinese representing the diverse communities that intersect in this neighborhood.

352 LANGUAGE OF THE BIRDS

353 POINT CLOUD

AT: MOSCONE CENTER
747 Howard Street
SoMa ③
illuminatesf.com

This illuminated 30-meter pedestrian bridge was designed by Leo Villareal, the same artist behind The Bay Lights. It features 28.000 overhead LED bulbs that change 30 times per second into many colors. The best viewing time is at night from the corner of Howard and Third Streets.

354 CITY HALL

1 Dr Carlton
B Goodlett Plaza
Civic Center ③
+1 415 554 4000
sfgov.org/cityhall

Since 2015 City Hall has become an architectural canvas of colorful lights and imagery. The digital projection system is city-owned and the building is often lit in a spectrum of colors to celebrate events and milestones, like rainbow hues in honor of Pride celebrations or orange when the SF Giants won the World Series.

355 NIGHT BLOOM

AT: CONSERVATORY
OF FLOWERS
100 John F.
Kennedy Drive
Golden Gate Park ⑥
+1 415 831 2090
*conservatoryof
flowers.org*

This stunning all-white landmark becomes a massive canvas for an evening light and sound show during special occasions of the year. The first one celebrated the Summer of Love's 50th Anniversary, and a couple of new ones have been created since. Check online to make sure there is a show before you go.

5 incredible

MASTERPIECES TO SEE FOR FREE

---

356 **'ALLEGORY OF CALIFORNIA' BY DIEGO RIVERA**
AT: THE CITY CLUB
155 Sansome Street
Financial District ②
sfcityguides.org

This is the first mural in America by the famous Mexican painter. It spans two floors and features Calafia, a fabled warrior queen who once ruled over the mythical island of California. To see it, you must sign up for a tour; reservations open 10 days before tour date.

357 **'THE THINKER' BY AUGUSTE RODIN**
AT: LEGION OF HONOR, LINCOLN PARK
100 34th Avenue
Sea Cliff ⑦
+1 415 750 3600
legionofhonor.famsf.org

One of the greatest works by one of the most legendary sculptors of all time. A number of casts were made of this piece and displayed in fine institutions around the globe. This one greets guests at the entrance of the Legion of Honor. Over 70 sculptures by the artist were purchased by local legend Alma Spreckels and donated to the museum.

358 'PAN AMERICAN UNITY MURAL' BY DIEGO RIVERA

AT: CITY COLLEGE OF
SAN FRANCISCO
50 Phelan Avenue
Sunnyside
+1 415 452 5188
riveramural.org

This is considered the most important work of art created in the Bay Area. This 7×22 meter fresco was commissioned in the 1940s for an international exposition in the city. Elements of art, religion, history and politics are combined with Diego's own self-portraits and one of his wife, artist Frida Kahlo.

359 'THE PIED PIPER OF HAMELIN' BY MAXFIELD PARRISH

AT: PALACE HOTEL
2 New Montgomery St
SoMa ③
+1 415 546 5089
piedpipersf.com

This piece by the renowned American painter has graced the hotel for over 100 years. It was commissioned for the reopening of the bar after the 1906 earthquake. In 2013 the hotel removed it to be sold at auction, outraging many patrons. After much rallying the hotel withdrew its intent to sell and the painting has remained since.

360 'THREE GEMS' BY JAMES TURRELL

AT: DE YOUNG MUSEUM
50 Hagiwara Tea
Garden Drive
Golden Gate Park ⑥
+1 415 750 3600
deyoung.famsf.org

In the sculpture garden is this subterranean designed by a legend in the light-and-space art movement. Enjoy the quiet space, allowing your eyes and mind to wander as clouds and birds pass the oculus above. The effects are subtle yet beautiful, but the real magic happens at twilight when colored lights appear and things become more noticeable.

5 quirky
PAINTED HOUSES
in SF

---

361 JUNGLE HOUSE
Church St betw
22nd and 23rd St
Noe Valley ⑤

Find every wild animal of the jungle painted onto this house in Noe Valley. They're all set against a lush backdrop of trees and waterfalls. And notice the extra details, like metal leaves sprouting from the treetops and the painted waste bins that perfectly blend into the scenery.

362 MONDRIAN HOUSE
Great Hwy betw
Rivera and
Quintara St
Outer Sunset ⑥

Fans of Dutch painter Piet Mondrian would appreciate this house. He was most known for his grid-based paintings which he started developing in 1919. They were composed of boxes in the shades of white, red, yellow and blue, all outlined in black. This house by the beach is painted in that style.

363 TIGER HOUSE
Frederick St near
Cole St
Cole Valley ⑥

Make your way to Cole Valley to see this uniquely painted house in the lushest shades of green. Here you'll encounter a large sprawling tiger peering at you from the jungle.

364 **HELIPAD HOUSE**

Folsom Street near
Ripley Street
Bernal Heights ⑤

The owner of the house worked with artist Casey O'Connell and allowed her to go wild on this painting. Her reason: 'Life's too short to live in a plain white house.' It features a sweet tattooed gal poking a shark in the eye. Look closely and see the city skyline in the shark's teeth.

365 **RAINBOW HOUSE**

Clipper St betw
Douglass and
Diamond St
Noe Valley ⑤

San Francisco is well known for its rainbow flags, but some homeowners took it much further and painted themselves a rainbow home. You'll find it in a quiet neighborhood and it's vibrantly painted in shades of red at the bottom to purples at the top.

364 HELIPAD HOUSE

5

ARTFUL STAIRWAYS
of SF

---

366 16TH AVENUE TILED STEPS
Moraga Street (betw 15th and 16th Ave)
Inner Sunset ⑥
16thavenuetiled steps.com

A beautiful mosaic runs along these 163 steps. It depicts life in the sea all the way up to the solar universe. Artists Aileen Barr and Colette Crutcher concepted the idea and neighbors joined to help and sponsor tiles within the mosaic. Start from the bottom, then enjoy the city view at the top.

367 FLIGHTS OF FANCY
Innes Avenue
Bayview/
Hunters Point

This 87-step staircase is a dedication to Dr. Arelious Walker, a former pastor and advocate of this neighborhood. The intricate design features textile and ceramic designs from various cultures, like cloth from Ghana, Native American pottery, and woven patterns from Central America and the Middle East.

368 LINCOLN PARK STEPS
California St and 32nd Ave
Outer Richmond ⑦
lincolnparksteps.org

A spectacular beaux-arts-inspired installation designed by local artist Aileen Barr. Previously it was a neglected stairwell and now it's something folks can enjoy for years to come. It's quiet and peaceful and close by are great attractions, like the Legion of Honor, Sutro Baths and Land's End.

369 **LYON STREET STEPS**

Lyon and Green Sts
Pacific Heights ①
Marina/Cow Hollow ①

Walk up or down these two perfectly-landscaped stairwells passing the most exclusive, multi-million-dollar homes of the city. In the middle is one of many heart sculptures displayed around the city. If you start from the bottom and reach the top, you'll also be rewarded with a breathtaking view of the city.

370 **HIDDEN GARDEN STEPS**

1515 16th Ave
(betw Kirkham and
Lawton St)
Inner Sunset ⑥
+1 415 621 3260
hiddengardensteps.org

This long stairwell is filled with a tile mosaic of beautiful flora and the garden creatures that inhabit it, like snails and butterflies. The bench at the bottom of the stairs is also painted. Nearby are the 16th Avenue Tiled Step, so you can squeeze both in one visit.

368 LINCOLN PARK STEPS

5 meccas for the
PERFORMING ARTS

---

371 BILL GRAHAM CIVIC AUDITORIUM

99 Grove Street
Civic Center ③
billgrahamcivic.com

This auditorium was built in 1915 for the Panama-Pacific International Exposition. It was named after the late Bill Graham, who began the rock 'n' roll movement in San Francisco in the 1960s. The building has hosted many important historic events since, and today it is the site for hundreds of concerts and special events.

372 DAVIES SYMPHONY HALL

201 Van Ness Avenue
Civic Center ③
+1 415 621 6600
sfwmpac.org/davies-symphony-hall

Home of the SF Symphony with performances, concerts and guest speakers scheduled throughout the year. It's for lovers of Mozart, Bach and Beethoven, as well as for movie-goers, as they often perform musical scores while screening the film. The curved glass lobby offers sweeping views of nearby City Hall and the Opera House.

373 SFJAZZ CENTER

201 Franklin Street
Hayes Valley ④
+1 866 920 5299
sfjazz.org

This expansive space is dedicated to jazz, as well as related forms of music and education, and performances are scheduled almost every day of the year. It was expertly designed to combine the acoustic quality of a great concert hall and the intimacy of a jazz club. You'll see and feel close to the performers wherever you're seated.

374 SHN ORPHEUM THEATRE

1192 Market Street
Civic Center ③
+1 888 746 1799
shnsf.com

Experience Broadway without having to venture to Broadway. It's the place to catch all the best (and often sold out) Tony-award winning performances, like *Hamilton, Book of Mormon, Phantom of the Opera, Les Miserables* and countless others. The theatre, which first opened in 1926, is also a historic city landmark.

375 WAR MEMORIAL PERFORMING ARTS CENTER

401 Van Ness Avenue
Civic Center ③
+1 415 621 6600
sfwmpac.org/war-memorial-opera-house

Opened in 1932, this exquisite beaux-arts structure is home to the San Francisco Opera and San Francisco Ballet. See the latest production of classics like *Carmen* and *Tosca*, and newly choreographed renditions of *Swan Lake* and *The Nutcracker*. And be sure to dress your best when visiting.

5 intimate venues to hear
LIVE MUSIC

376 **AMNESIA**
853 Valencia Street
Mission ⑤
amnesiathebar.com

This dim, red-lit music and beer hall hosts live entertainment – from singer songwriters to comedians – and serves a good variety of craft beers on tap every night of the week. A very intimate place to check out some local musical talent and sample brews from the West Coast.

377 **BLACK CAT**
400 Eddy Street
Tenderloin ③
+1 415 358 1999
blackcatsf.com

A very sexy, intimate jazz joint that's also a supper club. Think black brick walls, candelabras and plush velvet seating. Indulge in shared plates and sip on craft cocktails while enjoying nightly performances on stage, which is set very close to the dining area. The neighborhood may seem gritty, but this place is a gem.

378 BOTTOM OF THE HILL

1233 17th Street
Potrero Hill ⑤
+1 415 626 4455
bottomofthehill.com

They claim *Rolling Stone* chose them as 'the best place to hear live music in San Francisco'. And I agree it's a good one. The musical acts span from alternative to punk, and folk to hip-hop. Plus they have a full bar (it's cash only), a kitchen that's open late plus an outdoor patio area.

379 SWEDISH AMERICAN HALL AND CAFE DU NORD

2174 Market Street
Duboce Triangle ⑤
+1 415 471 2969
swedishamerican hall.com

This historic landmark built in 1907 was originally a meeting place for Swedish Americans. It has preserved its architectural charm and is now a music venue hosting larger performances and gatherings. The smaller, more intimate Cafe du Nord in the subterranean below has hosted musical acts for many years.

380 REVOLUTION CAFE

53248 22nd Street
Mission ⑤
+1 415 642 0474
revolutioncafesf.com

This lively European-style cafe opens out into the street and hosts live performances seven nights a week. No frills – it's a fun neighborhood place to unwind, listen to music, have a drink and people watch. It is cash only so be prepared.

5

CLASSIC CINEMAS

to catch a film

---

381 CASTRO THEATRE
429 Castro Street
Castro ⑤
+1 415 621 6120
castrotheatre.com

This theater was built in 1922 and is SF Historic Landmark #100. It's also one of the few remaining and still operating movie palaces in the country from the 1920s. The façade is reminiscent of a Mexican basilica and the interior is just as ornate. Catch a classic, the latest flick or join one of the fun musical sing-alongs.

382 ROXIE
3117 16th Street
Mission ⑤
+1 415 863 1087
roxie.com

Opened in 1909, this intimate 300-seat theater is the oldest continuously operating cinema in the country and the second oldest in the world. It has hosted every aspect of cinema and they 'strive to keep the weird and wonderful alive in our little corner of San Francisco' with unique indies, short films and festivals.

383 VOGUE THEATRE
3290 Sacramento St
Pacific Heights ①
+1 415 346 2228
voguesf.com

Coming in as the second oldest cinema in San Francisco, the Vogue Theatre opened in 1910. For over 100 years it has continuously hosted a run of foreign and independent films and it also happens to be the city's most popular venue for Woody Allen films.

384 PRESIDIO THEATRE

2340 Chestnut Street
Marina/Cow Hollow ①
+1 415 776 2988
lntsf.com/presidio

Owner Frank Lee has always loved movies, even working in the entertainment industry when he was just 11 years old. Later he established his own company, owning and operating three independent theaters in SF, including this one which opened in 1937. It is now a multiplex.

385 CLAY THEATRE

2261 Fillmore Street
Pacific Heights ①
+1 415 561 9921
landmarktheatres.com

This theatre was built in 1910 by the Naify brothers, builders of the first movie screen in town. In 1972 it hosted the first midnight movie in the city and continues that tradition to this day with cult favorites, like *The Rocky Horror Picture Show*. Recent independent films are screened here.

384 PRESIDIO THEATRE

5 places for
BIBLIOPHILES

---

386 ARION PRESS AND M & H TYPE

1802 Hays Street
Presidio ①
+1 415 668 2542
arionpress.com

Lovers of books and binding, font, type and machinery will truly enjoy this place. A tour is a must, especially to see the foundry below where the machinery, walls of typefaces and materials are housed. Tours are held Thursdays at 3.30 pm, require a reservation and cost 10 dollars.

387 THE BOOK CLUB OF CALIFORNIA

312 Sutter Street,
Suite 500
Union Square ③
+1 415 781 7532
bccbooks.org

In 1912, four men proposed a rare books and printing exhibit at the 1915 Panama-Pacific International Exposition. The concept was approved and they dubbed themselves the 'Book Club of California'. The exhibit never happened, but membership grew and their clubhouse boasts an impressive collection.

388 MECHANICS' INSTITUTE LIBRARY & CHESS ROOM

57 Post Street
Financial District ③
+1 415 393 0101
milibrary.org

The oldest library on the West Coast and the oldest chess club in the U.S. Founded in 1854, the book collection has grown beyond the technical to include other subjects, like business and the arts. Chess players of all ages and skill are welcome. It's free to visit and they offer a tour each Wednesday at noon.

389 PRELINGER LIBRARY
301 8th Street,
Room 215
SoMa ③
+1 415 252 8166
prelingerlibrary.org

This library isn't like most. Instead of traditional catalogs, materials are organized in a way that emphasizes browsing and discovering something new. The collection is mainly 19th- and 20th-century books, periodicals, maps and ephemera from the U.S. It's open to all for research, reading, inspiration and users can reuse images and text from the collection in their own projects.

390 SAN FRANCISCO CENTER FOR THE BOOK
375 Rhode Island St
Potrero Hill ⑤
+1 415 565 0545
sfcb.org

This organization is dedicated to the art and craft of the book, including letterpress printing, book binding and artists book-making. A great place to learn the history of books or get hands-on at one of their 400 workshops held annually. They also host free public programs like exhibits, book release parties, lectures and tours.

386 ARION PRESS AND M & H TYPE

5 cool places for
CURIOUS MINDS

---

391 **CAMERA OBSCURA**
1096 Point Lobos Ave
Sea Cliff ⑦
+1 415 750 0415

Peek at photography long before digital devices existed. This working camera obscura, a technique used as early as the Renaissance, reflects images of the beach front outside. The perfect time to visit is before sunset. The camera was originally part of the amusement park Playland that once occupied this area.

392 **THE INTERVAL
AT LONG NOW**
AT: FORT MASON CENTER
2 Marina Boulevard
Marina/Cow Hollow ①
theinterval.org

This bar, cafe and museum is also home to The Long Now, a society dedicated to ensuring humans stick around for a very long time. Floor-to-ceiling shelves contain thousands of books most needed to sustain and rebuild civilization in the event of an apocalypse. Center is a clock built to last 10.000 years.

393 LABYRINTHS & YOGA AT GRACE CATHEDRAL

1100 California St
Nob Hill ②
+1 415 749 6300
gracecathedral.org

Experience a candlelit walking meditation or participate in the Tuesday evening yoga sessions held on the labyrinths inside SF's most iconic cathedral. A unique opportunity to calm the mind and enjoy peace, quiet and reflection. Check the calendar for details and to sign up for these events.

394 PEEPHOLE CINEMA

280 Orange Alley
Mission ⑤
peepholecinema.com

Keep your eye out for this tiny theater hidden within this alleyway. It's literally a hole-in-the-wall. For those curious enough to find it, peer through the peephole and watch a stream of short silent films day or night. For safety in any alley, visit during the daytime unless you're with a group of friends.

395 SAN FRANCISCO COLUMBARIUM

One Loraine Court
Inner Richmond ⑦
+1 415 771 0717

Tucked in a residential cul-de-sac is this exquisite gem serving as the final resting place for many. Built in 1897, then abandoned, it was restored to its full glory towards the end of the 20th century. Peer through each glass niche (many incredibly decorated) for a glimpse into the lives of those interred there – from the 1890s to present.

KORET CHILDREN'S QUARTER PLAYGROUND

35 THINGS TO DO
WITH CHILDREN

———

5 great
TOY SHOPS

396 AMBASSADOR TOYS

2 Embarcadero
Center
Embarcadero ②
+1 415 345 8697
ambassadortoys.com

Though much smaller than the chain stores, this one offers a great selection of quality toys, especially many of the favorite classics. It's a great spot to get gifts for kids downtown, and if you're in a hurry, they provide quick and free gift wrapping.

397 TANTRUM

397 TANTRUM

858 Cole Street
Cole Valley ⑥
+1 415 504 6980
shoptantrum.com

Such a brilliant name for a children's shop. This circus and carnival-themed store carries a fun and colorful mix of kid-centric mid-century toys, clothing, jewelry, kitchenware, decor and other goodies and gifts, both new and vintage. There are a handful of things to delight adults, too. A second shop is in the Inner Richmond.

398 JEFFREY'S TOYS

A5 Kearny Street
Union Square ③
+1 415 291 8697
jeffreys.toys

The most enduring toy shop in the city, Jeffrey's has been family-owned and operated since 1966. In 2015 the shop had to vacate the space it occupied for 50 years and it reopened just blocks from their original location. It is reportedly one of the inspirations behind the Pixar film *Toy Story*.

399 MAPAMUNDI KIDS

1306 Castro Street
Noe Valley ⑤
+1 415 641 6192
mapamundikids.com

A truly distinctive and design-focused collection of toys, clothing, books and other lifestyle goods sourced globally for children and their discerning parents. Find unique books and quality-made toys of the wooden and fabric kind as opposed to plastic ones you'd find in most kids shops.

400 STANDARD 5 AND 10

3545 California St
Presidio Heights ①
+1 415 751 5767
standard5n10.com

One of the best collections of toys and games can be found in this one-stop variety shop, open since 1939. Two aisles are filled with great selections. Pick up other home- and hardware essentials while you're here.

5 shops
SPECIALIZING IN KIDS STUFF

401 ALDEA HOME + BABY
890 Valencia Street
Mission ⑤
+1 866 402 5332
aldeababy.com

This large shop not only has furnishings, clothing, toys and gear for babies and kids, but plenty of selections for the rest of your home, too. Especially if you are looking for things more unique, modern and vibrant in design.

402 SPROUT
1828 Union Street
Marina/Cow Hollow ①
+1 415 359 9205
sproutsanfrancisco.com

For those specifically seeking all-natural and organic products, clothing, toys and furnishings for their little ones, you'll find a wonderful but more limited selection here. They also host classes children can participate in – like sing-alongs and dance.

403 FIDDLESTICKS
540 Hayes Street
Hayes Valley ④
+1 415 565 0508
shopfiddlesticks.com

A shop that knows kids want to have fun and should have fun things to wear while they're at it, too. The selections, including apparel, toys and books, are colorful and feature whimsy characters to inspire their creativity. Let your kids' imaginations run wild and free.

404 MUDPIE

2185 Fillmore Street
Pacific Heights ①
+1 415 771 9262
mudpie-sf.com

At first glance you'd think it was a children's store, but it is so much more. The focus is mainly clothing and toys for the little folk, but for the elder ones, the offerings have expanded to include home decor, furnishings, apothecary goods, books and kitchen accessories – both vintage and new.

405 MONKEI MILES

1601 Irving Street
Inner Sunset ⑥
+1 415 650 3031

Children outgrow their clothing and toys quickly, and the money spent to keep buying them new things add up. So here's a sweet consignment shop to sell or purchase gently worn and used kids' items at affordable prices. It's good for the wallet and the environment.

5

INDOOR PLACES
kids will love

---

406 CIRCUS CENTER

755 Frederick Street
Inner Sunset ⑥
+1 415 759 8123
circuscenter.org

Has your kid ever dreamt of running away with the circus? They can or at least learn some of the tricks required to. You can register them for playtime in their circus playground or sign them up for a program or camp. They'll learn trapeze, trampoline, juggling, tumbling and rope climbing, too.

407 CHILDREN'S CREATIVITY MUSEUM

221 Fourth Street
SoMa ③
+1 415 820 3320
creativity.org

There are many activities here allowing your children to run wild with their imagination. The programs and exhibits will keep them entertained for hours, including walls of Legos and magnets, robots, trains, the music video studio, animation and tech rooms, and the foam block area among many others.

408 HOUSE OF AIR

926 Mason Street
Presidio ①
+1 415 345 9675
houseofair.com

A warehouse dedicated to air-based activities like trampoline, trampoline dodgeball, rock climbing and slack-lining. Take the kids here and watch them jump, jump and jump. There is a mini trampoline court dedicated to just them. Let them bounce around and burn off all that kid energy.

409 THE RANDALL MUSEUM

199 Museum Way
Corona Heights ⑤
+1 415 554 9600
randallmuseum.org

This museum for families, children and teens is focused on science, nature and art. They offer a great number of drop-in activities, classes, camps and field trips throughout the year. Kids especially love their small animals and learning about trains and cable cars here. Admission is free but be kind and leave a donation.

410 MUSÉE MÉCANIQUE

Pier 45, at the end
of Taylor Street,
Shed A
Fisherman's Wharf ②
+1 415 346 2000
museemecaniquesf.com

Get ready to drop quarters into this collection of over 200 coin-operated mechanical musical instruments and antique arcade machines. Many of these, like Laffing Sal and The Arm Wrestler, came from the Cliff House, where the old Playland amusement park (1913-1972) once occupied that part of the beach.

5

OUTDOOR PLACES

kids will love

---

411 SEWARD STREET SLIDES

30 Seward Street
Eureka Valley ⑤

For some real free fun, head to these concrete slides. And use the cardboard that's left behind. It's a steep climb, so wear proper clothing and shoes (no skirts, dresses and sandals). Then sit on your board and slide on down. Open Tuesday through Sunday from 10 am to 5 pm and closed on Mondays.

412 STOW LAKE BOATHOUSE

50 Stow Lake Drive
Golden Gate Park ⑥
+1 415 702 1390
stowlakeboathouse.com

Rent a boat with your little ones and enjoy the sight of turtles and ducks as they go swimming by. You have a choice of a paddle or pedal boat and each rents by the hour. There is a cafe with snacks, but it's great to bring your own.

413 GOLDEN GATE PARK CAROUSEL

Koret Children's
Quarter located off
of Kezar Drive
Golden Gate Park ⑥
+1 415 231 0077
goldengatepark.com/
childrens-playground

Take a whirl with all the magical creatures on this historic carousel designed by New York company, Herschell-Spillman in 1912. It is open daily and adults and children can ride for a small fee. Look closely inside the carousel and you'll find painted panels that illustrate the region's landscapes.

414 BAY AREA DISCOVERY MUSEUM

557 McReynolds Rd
Sausalito
+1 415 339 3900
bayareadiscovery
museum.org

An innovative, mostly outdoors museum for kids with an unbeatable location right under the Sausalito side of the Golden Gate Bridge. They have fun exhibits, events, classes and camps designed to transform the way children learn as they play. The playground here is a hit. You can bring your own snacks.

415 SAN FRANCISCO ZOO

1 Zoo Road
Lakeshore
+1 415 753 7080
sfzoo.org

The zoo is home to over 2000 exotic, endangered and rescued animals. It's an opportunity to get close to animals from all parts of the world with the hope that the interaction here leads to conservation action for wildlife everywhere. They offer camps and classes for children of all ages.

412 STOW LAKE BOATHOUSE

5 of the best
PLAYGROUNDS
in SF

---

416 HELEN DILLER PLAYGROUND

19th and Dolores St
Mission ⑤
sfrecpark.org/project/
mission-dolores-
park-helen-diller-
playground

This may be the largest playground in San Francisco. It offers many slides, swing and rope structures on a rubber floor for safe landings. Adults can play on many of these, too. Even better, it has a spectacular view of the city and there's an ice-cream shop close by for a sweet treat.

417 JULIUS KAHN PLAYGROUND

Pacific Ave and
Spruce St
Presidio Heights ①
sfrecpark.org/
destination/julius-
kahn-playground

This gated playground offers swings, good climbing structures and a baseball and soccer field. You are surrounded by beautiful trees and you can see the Golden Gate Bridge on a clear day. It's also nearby walking trails to explore other parts of the Presidio.

418 LAFAYETTE PLAYGROUND

Clay St at Laguna St
Pacific Heights ①
sfrecpark.org/
destination/
lafayette-park

One of the more creative play areas with unique slides (in the form of tubes and wiggly lines), rope ladders and bridges, and a large water play area for splashing and filling up water guns. A big hit on warmer days. The playground is perched on a hill, so you also get wraparound views of the city.

419 MISSION BAY CHILDREN'S PARK

Long Bridge and
El Dorado St
Mission Bay ③
missionbayparks.com

This enclosed playground offers unique climbing structures and walls, crazy looking huts to run through, modern see-saws, merry-go-rounds and a sand pit and area for water play. There is a nice grassy area for picnics and it's close to food trucks at nearby Spark Social.

420 KORET CHILDREN'S QUARTER PLAYGROUND

320 Bowling Green
Drive
Golden Gate Park ⑥
sfrecpark.org/
destination/golden-
gate-park/koret-
childrens-quarter

This large playground is located inside Golden Gate Park and features many play areas for children of all ages. There are concrete slides, plenty of swings, zip lines, a spider web-like climbing tower and an old carousel, too. And many grassy knolls for picnicking.

5 spots to
GRAB A SCOOP

---

421 MR. AND MRS. MISCELLANEOUS

699 22nd Street
Dogpatch ⑤
+1 415 970 0750

A fantastic ice-cream shop with a blackboard menu of distinctive flavors for the day. The sauces and toppings are also made in-house. Add some to your scoops. There are bags of peanut butter malt balls and jars of brittles you can buy here, too.

422 SMITTEN

432 Octavia Street
Hayes Valley ④
+1 415 863 1518
smittenicecream.com

It's like a mad scientist lab with smoke erupting from metal spinning machines. Watch as clumps are formed, then balled into the smoothest and creamiest ice cream ever created. The science is in the liquid nitrogen that is used to freeze the treat. Kids go wild over the smoky action.

423 THE ICE CREAM BAR

815 Cole Street
Cole Valley
+1 415 742 4932
theicecreambarsf.com

This place is a blast from the past. You'll feel as if you've walked into a classic 1930s diner with its lunch counter, soda fountain and 'jerks' serving up ice cream, malts, milkshakes, floats, and the best part: handcrafted sodas made-to-order the old fashioned way using a blend of extracts, acids and soda water.

424 BI-RITE CREAMERY

3692 18th Street
Mission ⑤
+1 415 626 5600
biritemarket.com/
creamery

This creamery offers ice-cream scoops, soft serves, sundaes, cakes, bars, sandwiches and filled donuts. Nearby is Dolores Park, so after a day at the playground, stop here for a sweet treat. It's a popular spot, so be prepared to wait in the long line.

425 TWIRL AND DIP

Check website
for locations in
Golden Gate Park ⑥
+1 415 205 8261
twirlanddip.com

Spot this ice-cream truck in Golden Gate Park. It's usually positioned near the Japanese Tea Garden, but check online in case it moves locations. It's organic soft serve ice cream that can be dipped in dark chocolate and sprinkled with handmade sauces and toppings. It's much better than the ones we had as kids.

422 SMITTEN

5 spots to
GRAB A SWEET TREAT

---

426 ANTHONY'S COOKIES
1417 Valencia Street
Mission ⑤
+1 415 655 9834
anthonyscookies.com

Order not just one or two but a whole box full as you'll want more to enjoy later. These are the best chocolate chip cookies in the city. They're perfectly bite-sized and come in a dozen other varieties. And yes, they have milk, too.

427 KARA'S CUPCAKES
3249 Scott Street
Marina/Cow Hollow ①
+1 866 554 2253
karascupcakes.com

Delicious, freshly baked cupcakes and cakes made by hand in small batches using fine ingredients sourced locally and organically whenever possible. The treats quickly became a big hit and multiple locations have opened up throughout the city and Bay Area. This is the original location.

428 MIETTE
449 Octavia Street
Hayes Valley ④
+1 415 626 6221
miette.com

This is the sweetest, most cheeriest shop in the city. The walls are filled with jars of candies, gummies, licorice and confections from all parts of the world. Packages of homemade cookies and caramels are lined on trays, and freshly baked macarons, cakes and cupcakes tempt you from the case.

429 THE CANDY STORE

1507 Vallejo Street
Russian Hill ②
+1 415 921 8000
thecandystoresf.com

This darling boutique has walls lined with old-fashioned candy jars, each filled with gummies, sours, sweets and all kinds of confections from around the world. And some classic old treats you probably haven't seen in years.

430 DEVIL'S TEETH BAKING COMPANY

3876 Noriega Street
Outer Sunset ⑥
+1 415 683 5533
devilsteethbaking
company.com

Kids (and adults, too) will love the pastries, sweets and savories at this joint located close to the beach. They have good old classics, like brownies and lemon bars, plus fun ones, like the donut muffins and shark-shaped cookies. On weekends they have breakfast sandwiches and 1 dollar beignets on Sundays.

428 MIETTE

SAN FRANCISCO PROPER HOTEL

30 PLACES
TO SLEEP

---

5 unique
BOUTIQUE HOTELS

---

431 HOTEL G

386 Geary Street
Union Square ③
+1 415 986 2000
hotelgsanfrancisco.com

Centrally located, beautifully decorated, affordable and with great amenities. The hotel also serves a gallery with artwork displayed in each of the rooms and public areas. All are available for purchase and benefit a wonderful local organization that supports artists with developmental disabilities.

432 PHOENIX HOTEL

601 Eddy Street
Tenderloin ③
+1 415 776 1380
phoenixsf.com

A vibrant hotel with a tropical-retro vibe plus heated pool in the midst of the city. There is also a restaurant on site for dinner, cocktails and weekend brunch, served inside or poolside on the patio. They often host DJs and special events, so this place is ideal for those seeking a party.

433 HOTEL ZETTA

55 5th Street
SoMa ③
+1 415 543 8555
viceroyhotelsand
resorts.com/en/zetta

An artsy hotel with fun features, including a lounge with Alcatraz prisoner mugshots, a chandelier made of eyeglasses and stairwells lined with graffiti. The Playroom on the second level offers many game options plus a wall-size plinko that drops into the main lobby.

434 HOTEL TRITON

342 Grant Avenue
Union Square ③
+1 844 808 0290
hoteltriton.com

Opened in 1913, this cool and quirky hotel has the cheeriest, most colorful lobby imaginable. Very boho-chic. Rooms are wallpapered with pages from Jack Kerouac's *On the Road*, and suites are themed, like the Haagen-Dazs 'Sweet Suite' with unlimited ice cream and the 'J. Garcia Suite' designed by the Grateful Dead frontman himself.

435 HOTEL VERTIGO

940 Sutter Street
Lower Nob Hill ③
+1 415 885 6800
haiyi-hotels.com/
hotelvertigosf

Alfred Hitchcock fans will recognize this as the 'Empire Hotel' where Judy (Kim Novak's character) lived in the classic thriller *Vertigo*. It was partially filmed at this location. Today the movie is played on a loop behind the reception desk and you can experience a bit of vertigo by looking down the winding stairwell from high above.

431 | HOTEL G

5 of the hippest
DESIGN HOTELS

436 STAYPINEAPPLE

580 Geary Street
Union Square ③
+1 415 441 2700
staypineapple.com/
union-square-
san-francisco

There is a pineapple theme here – from the key cards to the coffee pods in your room to the cupcakes served each day. Each room is bright, beautifully designed and clean. So clean that their 'Naked Experience' assures you can sleep in the nude. Be sure to visit their Pineapple Bistro and Bar to fuel up during your visit.

437 AXIOM HOTEL

28 Cyril Magnin St
Union Square ③
+1 415 392 9466
axiomhotel.com

This chic hotel provides a modern and eco-friendly experience. First you enter a living room library and check-in. In your room, you can mirror your mobile device to the television. Shampoo and soap are in pump dispensers and each floor has a water filtration system. And the second floor provides communal work spaces and arcade games.

438 HOTEL VIA

138 King Street
South Beach ③
+1 415 200 4977
hotelviasf.com

Located across from the ballpark is this hotel for those who prefer a modern, minimalist aesthetic. The views from select rooms and the rooftop lounge look out towards the park and waterfront. The lounge (with private cabanas, fire pits, heat lamps and bar) is available exclusively to guests.

439 SAN FRANCISCO PROPER HOTEL

1100 Market Street
Tenderloin ③
+1 415 735 7777
properhotel.com/
hotels/san-francisco

The newest and chicest property to hit the city. This old hotel has been completely revised and given a modern interior makeover by design extraordinaire Kelly Wearstler. Each room is styled with her signature flair and lounges have an eclectic mix of artwork. Enjoy stylish drinks and food from both the lobby and must-see rooftop bar.

440 THE ST. REGIS SAN FRANCISCO

125 3rd Street
SoMa ③
+1 415 284 4000
stregissanfrancisco.com

Stylish, sophisticated and truly relaxing. First impression as you step into an expansive lounge and lobby bar warmed by an indoor fireplace. Each guestroom is designed in soft shades and equipped with beautiful amenities creating a very soothing environment. Many rooms have oversized soaking tubs. There is also a pool and spa on site.

5 hotels that offer
ROOMS WITH A VIEW

---

441 ARGONAUT HOTEL

495 Jefferson Street
Fisherman's Wharf ②
+1 800 790 1415
argonauthotel.com

Located a block from the waterfront, this seaside-inspired hotel looks right out to Alcatraz, the bay and to Fisherman's Wharf below. Of course, you'll have to pay extra for rooms with views. Otherwise you're a quick skip from these and many other points of interests.

442 FAIRMONT HERITAGE PLACE

900 North Point St
Fisherman's Wharf ②
+1 415 268 9900
fairmont.com/
ghirardelli-san-
francisco

Enjoy sweeping views of the bay from this hotel located atop historic Ghirardelli Square and site of the original chocolate factory. Watch the fog roll in and catch glimpses of the Golden Gate Bridge, Alcatraz and the activity in the courtyards below. The outdoor terraces are equipped with fire pits for chilly mornings and nights.

443 HOTEL VITALE

8 Mission Street
Embarcadero ②
+1 415 278 3700
jdvhotels.com/hotels/
california

A luxury boutique hotel with stunning views of the Embarcadero waterfront, which can be seen from almost every room. You can head to the rooftop or penthouse spa for even better views. The interiors are clean, modern and simple, and the hotel is conveniently located next to great sites and restaurants.

444 INTERCONTINENTAL MARK HOPKINS

999 California Street
Nob Hill ②
+1 415 392 3434
intercontinental
markhopkins.com

This landmark luxury property offers remarkable views from the tippy top of Nob Hill. And surrounding it are some of the most beautiful buildings with rich architecture. The penthouse lounge known as the Top of the Mark offers food and drinks with a 360-degree view of the city.

445 LOEWS REGENCY

222 Sansome Street
Financial District ②
+1 844 327 7098
loewshotels.com/
regency-san-francisco

This hotel occupies the top 11 floors of a 48-story building, so guaranteed you'll get commanding views of the city from high up here. You have a choice of city or bay view rooms and suites. Head up to the sky deck for a 'Spirits in the Sky' cocktail experience.

5

HISTORIC HOTELS
in SF

---

446 FAIRMONT

950 Mason Street
Nob Hill ②
+1 415 772 5000
fairmont.com/
san-francisco

One of the grand dames of Nob Hill, this luxury hotel has had its share of historical moments. It is here where the United Nations Charter was drafted in 1945 and where Tony Bennett first sang *I Left My Heart in San Francisco* in 1961. His statue stands outside the hotel.

447 HOTEL MAJESTIC

1500 Sutter Street
Pacific Heights ①
+1 415 441 1100
thehotelmajestic.com

Built in 1902 by the Schmitt Family, this hotel remained unscathed by the 1906 devastation. It's the longest operating hotel in SF and has kept its original architecture, styled with Victorian and Edwardian accents. Rumor has it, one of Milton Schmitt's daughters haunts the hotel to this day – especially the fourth floor.

448 PALACE HOTEL

2 New Montgomery St
SoMa ③
+1 415 512 1111
sfpalace.com

An icon since 1875, The Palace is the city's first luxury hotel. It has maintained its original architecture and decorative elements while updating its guest rooms to a modern elegance. Enjoy tea service under the golden chandeliers in the Garden Court and visit the *Pied Piper of Hamelin* by artist Maxfield Parrish in the lounge.

449 THE RITZ-CARLTON

600 Stockton Street
Chinatown ②
+1 415 296 7465
ritzcarlton.com

This 1909 architectural gem and historic landmark sits atop Chinatown. The façade is neoclassical and reminiscent of a Greek temple, while the interior is modern and luxurious in design. The hotel has earned all the major accolades in hospitality, so expect top-notch service and amenities during your stay here.

450 THE WESTIN ST. FRANCIS

335 Powell Street
Union Square ③
+1 415 397 7000
westin.com/
sanfrancisco

The St. Francis maintains many traditions since opening in 1904. It was a popular place to convene and folks would tell others to 'meet at the clock'. The original timepiece remains in the lobby. They offer the world's only silver coin cleaning service, a custom since 1938 to keep ladies' white gloves from getting dirty.

448 PALACE HOTEL

5
VICTORIAN HOMES
to stay in

---

451 THE CHATEAU TIVOLI
1057 Steiner Street
Alamo Square ④
+1 415 776 5462
chateautivoli.com

This is the most exquisite Victorian to stay in from the inside and out. The townhouse was built in 1892 and boasts nine lavishly appointed rooms and suites. Beautiful estate pieces were sourced to adorn the parlors and dining room. And included with your stay are breakfast, wine and cheese, and coffee and tea service.

452 THE GROVE INN
890 Grove Street
Hayes Valley ④
+1 415 929 0780
groveinnsf.com

Originally built as a Gold Rush boarding house in the 1800s, this Italianate-Victorian style inn is located just one block away from Alamo Square and the famous Painted Ladies. Each room is simple and elegantly decorated and stays come with complimentary breakfast each morning. Major sites, restaurants and shopping are within walking distance.

453 THE INN SAN FRANCISCO

943 South
Van Ness Avenue
Mission ⑤
+1 415 641 0188
innsf.com

Enjoy a bed and breakfast stay at this elegant, richly decorated Victorian built on what was called Mansion Row in the 1870s. Each room is truly unique in style. Bonus is a garden patio, rooftop sundeck and hot tub. It's located in the Mission district close to many restaurants and sites.

454 JACKSON COURT

2198 Jackson Street
Pacific Heights ①
+1 415 929 7670
jacksoncourt.com

This brownstone Victorian was built in 1900 and is located in the prestigious Pacific Heights neighborhood. The ten guest rooms are furnished in a traditional style, including antique carved wooden beds. Nearby are two major pedestrian streets full of restaurants, cafes and boutiques. There are great city views from the top of the hill here.

455 THE PARSONAGE

198 Haight Street
Hayes Valley ④
+1 415 863 3699
theparsonage.com

An 1883 Historic Landmark Victorian home elegantly designed with American and European antiques. The home features five guest rooms, two parlors, a library and a dining room where guests can enjoy a multi-course breakfast plus treats in the evening. Its location is within walking distance to the great shops and eateries of Hayes Valley.

5 hotels to
ESCAPE THE HUSTLE AND BUSTLE

456 CAVALLO POINT

601 Murray Circle
Sausalito
+1 855 730 6984
cavallopoint.com

Just across and right below the Golden Gate Bridge is this beautiful historic property that was formerly a U.S. Army post. Old officers' residences have since been converted into luxury guest rooms, a restaurant and a spa. The only things surrounding you are trees and the bay, so expect the most quiet and serene getaway.

457 INN AT THE PRESIDIO

42 Moraga Avenue
(on Main Post)
Presidio ①
+1 415 800 7356
innatthepresidio.com

Inside this sprawling old military post is the Presidio's only hotel. The area is full of winding roads, trees and sparsely placed homes and buildings, so it doesn't get much quieter than this. This elegant property was once home to bachelor officers in the Army, and now it's a lodge with 22 luxurious and spacious accommodations.

458 HOTEL DRISCO

2901 Pacific Avenue
Pacific Heights ①
+1 800 634 7277
hoteldrisco.com

Plan a stay at this elegant 1903 Edwardian hotel located in the city's poshest neighborhood. It blends right in with other fine homes on the hilltops, making it a perfect and quiet hideaway. Stepping out of the hotel you'll feel like a local. And from this high up, the views are remarkable.

459 HOTEL KABUKI

1625 Post Street
Japantown ④
+1 415 922 3200
jdvhotels.com

Head to peaceful Japantown for a stay at this newly renovated hotel that combines a bit of East and West. Rooms are adorned with modern furnishings, a soothing palette, and a plush bed. Wellness amenities include a beautiful redesigned gym and a meditation garden.

460 THE LAUREL INN

444 Presidio Avenue
Pacific Heights ①
+1 800 552 8735
jdvhotels.com

This one is in a residential neighborhood far from downtown and closer to areas like Golden Gate Park, Golden Gate Bridge and the Presidio. It feels more like a cozy apartment or studio than a hotel – many rooms come with kitchenettes. And you're within walking distance of boutique shops, cafes and restaurants.

40 THINGS TO DO ON THE WEEKEND

---

5 great
URBAN HIKES

461 LANDS END TRAIL

680 Point Lobos Ave
Sea Cliff ⑦
+1 415 426 5240
*parksconservancy.org/
parks/lands-end*

Start at the visitor center and venture on this 5,5-km trail with the most picturesque views of the coast. Wind your way through the cliffs and cypress trees while stopping at points like the old Sutro Bath ruins, Point Lobos, the Labyrinth and Mile Rock Beach.

462 GLEN CANYON PARK

Elk St and Cheney St
Glen Park ⑥
*sfrecpark.org/
destination/glen-park*

This is a very large wilderness park, so a good starting point is to begin at the recreation center and start the trails from there. They range from easy to challenging and along the way you'll encounter wildflowers, huge rock formations and beautiful views. It's quiet, desolate and a nice respite from the busy city.

463 FORT FUNSTON

Fort Funston Road
Lakeshore
+1 415 561 4323
*parksconservancy.org/
parks/fort-funston*

Explore the sandy bluffs along with the batteries and forts formerly built to protect the city from invasion during WWII. Efforts were abandoned and today there are many trails you can take to explore this area above the ocean. Watch hang-gliders soar off the cliffs or take the steep climb down to the beach.

464 BARBARY COAST TRAIL

START AT: THE SAN FRANCISCO MINT

88 5th Street
SoMa ③
+1 415 454 2355
barbarycoasttrail.org

Discover the city's legendary Gold Rush history by following the bronze medallions on this 6-km trail through the city. You'll visit twenty historic sites, including where sailors were 'shanghai-ed' and where Jack Kerouac liked to unwind and write. Start at The San Francisco Mint and wind your way to the waterfront.

465 BATTERIES TO BLUFFS TRAIL

The Presidio,
Langdon Court at
Battery Godfrey
Presidio ①
presidio.gov/trails/
batteries-to-bluffs-trail

Meander through the wild western shoreline of the Presidio and explore the old historic gun batteries, coastal plants and wildlife. The trail offers stunning ocean views from here. Expect steps and some moderate climbs plus a side trip down to the beach. The loop is about 3,7 km and a great one to do around sunset.

461 LANDS END TRAIL

5 places to
TAKE A WORKSHOP

466 1AM SF (FIRST AMENDMENT)

1000 Howard Street
SoMa ③
+1 888 589 0475
1amsf.com

This organization represents the freedom of speech through urban art exhibitions, public murals and experiences. Explore the works they have on display, or even better, sign up for a graffiti/street art walking tour or take a hands-on class to discover your own style and how to work with a spray can.

467 CLAY BY THE BAY

1618 Pacific Avenue
Nob Hill ②
+1 415 416 6475
claybythebaysf.com

Try your hand at the wheel at this expansive, multi-level pottery studio. Sign up for a one-day workshop or enroll in their six-week programs exploring the basics to more advanced techniques. They also teach hand building methods if you choose to skip the wheel.

468 GENERAL ASSEMBLY

225 Bush Street,
5th Floor
Financial District ②
+1 415 592 6885
generalassemb.ly/
locations/san-francisco

The Bay Area has been a hub for tech innovation. Is developing your skills in this field of interest? Sign up for coding, design, data, marketing and other business courses designed for entrepreneurs and start-ups. They offer full-time, part-time, one-time classes, workshops and often host special events. Check the listings online.

469 HARVEY MILK PHOTO CENTER

50 Scott Street
Haight-Ashbury ⑤
+1 415 554 9522
harveymilkphoto
center.org

Photography classes of all types are held throughout the week, from the basics of black and white to digital to software editing. A great way to learn or develop new skills. You can also sign up for courses where you explore and capture sites around the city, like hidden spots in Chinatown at night.

470 WORKSHOP

1798 McAllister St
NoPa ④
+1 415 874 9186
workshopsf.org

Learn watercolor, metalsmithing, jewelry making, woodworking, pickling and other hands-on crafts from local artists and makers. This facility offers affordable do-it-yourself classes for adults throughout the week. Some are one-day workshops and others are multi-day. There is a wide array of programs to choose from.

5 places to
TAKE A LOCAL COOKING CLASS

---

471 **18 REASONS**

3674 18th Street
Mission ⑤
+1 415 568 2710
18reasons.org

This organization provides its members and others in the community with the opportunity to buy, cook and eat good food every day through education and classes held each week. Sign up for a workshop to sharpen your skills in the kitchen, from knife training to making special dishes. See schedule online.

472 **LA COCINA**

2948 Folsom Street
Mission ⑤
+1 415 824 2729
lacocinasf.org

Learn to cook from many of the aspiring female food talent here. This incredible incubator assists low-income food entrepreneurs by providing commercial kitchen space, technical assistance and access to other services to launch and grow their food business. Class offerings can be viewed on their website.

473 **SAN FRANCISCO COOKING SCHOOL**

690 Van Ness Ave
Civic Center ③
+1 415 346 2665
sfcooking.com

By day the kitchen is dedicated to aspiring professionals building their culinary skills, and on evenings and weekends they open up for public cooking classes. Learn how to prepare specialty dishes (like *tamales* and dim sum) to holiday confections. Look up classes on their website.

474 THE CIVIC KITCHEN

2961 Mission Street
Mission ⑤
+1 415 429 2411
civickitchensf.com

This small cooking school offers workshops and events in a warm, welcoming space and kitchen. Several classes are offered weekly – from basic kitchen and knife skills to advanced culinary dishes. Browse through their wall of cookbooks for more inspiration while you're there. Check online for their schedule.

475 CUESA: CENTER FOR URBAN EDUCATION ABOUT SUSTAINABLE AGRICULTURE

1 Ferry Building,
Suite 50
Embarcadero ②
+1 415 291 3276
cuesa.org

These folks are dedicated to educating urban consumers about sustainable agriculture and does so through its weekly farmers markets and programs, like farm tours and cooking demonstrations. Chefs and other food artisans offer free demos at the markets and you can sign up for their low-cost hands-on culinary classes, like cheese and cocktail making.

5 easy
DAY TRIP DESTINATIONS
(within 45 minutes)

---

476 MARIN HEADLANDS

Take Highway 101
and the exit to Marin
Headlands
Sausalito
+1 415 561 4700
nps.gov/goga/marin-
headlands.htm

Cross the Golden Gate Bridge and explore the hilly peninsula that offers spectacular views of the bridge, city and the Pacific coastline. Pack some snacks, spot wild animals and wildflowers as you make your way up to Hawk Hill then down to Rodeo Beach, Point Bonita Lighthouse and Tennessee Valley.

477 PACIFICA TO PESCADERO

Take Highway 1 to
Pacifica State Beach
up to Pigeon Point
Lighthouse

There are many points of interests along this part of the California coast. Explore the many beaches, surf towns, lighthouses, wildlife reserve, seafood joints and farms. In Pescadero, head into town for their famous artichoke bread, meet the goats and taste cheese at Harley Farms, and visit the lighthouse.

477 PACIFICA TO PESCADERO

478 **MOUNT TAMALPAIS**

Take Highway 101 to Highway 1 towards Mount Tamalpais
Marin County
+1 415 388 2070
parks.ca.gov

Hike the golden grasslands to get to the summit or explore any of the surrounding trails that take you deep into forests and past some waterfalls. Then grab a bite at the English-style pub called the Pelican Inn or do the pancake hike over to West Point Inn (hosted second Sunday of the month from July to October).

479 **SONOMA**

Take Highway 101 to Highway 37 to Highway 121 towards Sonoma
Sonoma Valley

A short 45-minute drive gives you a first glimpse and taste of wine country. Wind your way through the many vineyards and sample the wines this region is known for. Some wineries require a reservation so plan ahead. Sonoma is an easy day trip or a perfect weekend stay to indulge a bit longer.

480 **STINSON TO BOLINAS**

Take Highway 1 to Stinson Beach and Bolinas

It's a long windy road to get to these two towns, but it's an incredible scenic experience. You'll make many stops to enjoy the ocean vistas. The beach at Stinson is perfect for picnicking while the one in Bolinas is great for fishing and surfing. Both towns have a handful of charming eateries to enjoy.

5 areas to
GO FOR A LONG RUN

---

481 EMBARCADERO
Embarcadero ② ③

From the ballpark, head north along the paved Embarcadero until you reach the end at Pier 45. This flat 5,5-km path will guide you along the waterfront past piers full of sites. If you want more of a challenge, continue past Fisherman's Wharf and over Fort Mason to get closer to the Golden Gate Bridge.

482 GOLDEN GATE BRIDGE
Presidio ①

A perfect way to experience this icon is to run across it and back. The span is 2,7 km, so a round trip run is about 5,5 km. No running on the biking side of the bridge, so you'll have to navigate around folks stopping to take photos on the walking side.

483 GOLDEN GATE PARK
Golden Gate Park ⑥

There are many entrances and routes you can take. It's a matter of where you want to start and what you want to see. The full length east to west is 5 km. North to south is about 0,8 km. On Sundays the park closes its roads and restricts cars for most of the day.

484 CRISSY FIELD TO HOPPER'S HANDS
Presidio ①

Starting at the east end of Crissy Field Beach, start running towards the Golden Gate Bridge. As you approach the bridge you'll see a chain-linked fence where the sidewalk ends. Look for the plaque with two hands and give it a high-five or fist bump before turning back around. It's been a tradition amongst runners for over 15 years. The roundtrip to and from is 5,5 km.

485 OCEAN BEACH
Outer Richmond ⑦
Outer Sunset ⑥

Starting at the Cliff House and ending at the San Francisco Zoo is a flat, no-incline 5-km run one way. You can opt for the paved road, or for more of a challenge, run right on the beach. Enjoy the cool ocean breeze and pass fishermen and surfers as you go by.

485 OCEAN BEACH

5 *fun ways to*
ENJOY THE SF BAY
BY WATER

---

486 BEACH CLEANUP WITH SURFRIDER FOUNDATION

Ocean Beach and Baker Beach
Sea Cliff ⑦
*sf.surfrider.org/
beach-cleanups*

Explore two of SF's beaches while helping the environment. Visitors and locals sign up for these popular beach cleanups that take place every other Sunday. Enjoy the beautiful scenic backdrop and make new friends while you're at it. Buckets and gloves are provided or you can bring your own.

487 CAPTAIN KIRK'S SAN FRANCISCO SAILING

Various pickup locations
+1 650 930 0740
sfbaysail.com

Explore the Bay aboard one of three yachts. You can participate in sailing the boats or sit back and enjoy the ride. Boats can be chartered for a few hours or for specific events, like a sunset sail or a barbeque on Angel Island.

488 DOLPHIN CLUB
AT: AQUATIC PARK

502 Jefferson St
Fisherman's Wharf ②
+1 415 441 9329
dolphinclub.org

Join the city's oldest swimming club where members have been braving the bone-chilling waters of the Bay in their swimsuits (wetsuits are not allowed) since 1877. Membership is required and strict rules need to be abided here. Swims are done in the cove and those who meet specific requirements can swim out to Alcatraz and the bridge.

489 SAN FRANCISCO WHALE TOURS

Pier 39
Fisherman's Wharf ②
+1 415 706 7364
sanfranciscowhale
tours.com

Head under the Golden Gate Bridge and far into the ocean in search of blue, gray and humpback whales. Keep your eyes open as you leave the Bay and head towards the Farallon Islands, a sanctuary of birds and other marine wildlife. Whales can be spotted all year round.

490 SEA TREK KAYAK & STAND UP PADDLE BOARD CENTER
AT: BAY MODEL

2100 Bridgeway
Sausalito
+1 415 332 8494
seatrek.com

Rent a kayak or stand-up paddle board any day of the week by the hour or sign up for a class. Explore different routes around the Sausalito waterfront where the water is much calmer than SF. You can also sign up for special occasion trips, like an evening kayak under a full moon.

5 places to
GO ANTIQUING

---

491 BIG DADDY'S ANTIQUES

1550 17th Street
Potrero Hill ⑤
+1 415 621 6800
bdantiques.com

A massive warehouse where everything antique, salvaged, industrial, and repurposed fills every nook and corner, from ceiling to floor. This is where you go if you are looking for something truly unique for your home or garden. And be sure to peep in on the live birds in the large vintage cages.

492 PAST PERFECT

6101 Geary Blvd
Outer Richmond ⑦
+1 415 929 2288
pastperfectsf.com

With two locations in the city and goods from more than thirty independent dealers, there are many one-of-a-kind treasures to be found. This space is the larger of the two. The selections of furniture, lighting, decor, art and fashion are ever-changing. Fans of mid-century modern design will enjoy the offerings here.

495 ALAMEDA POINT ANTIQUES FAIRE

493 TREASUREFEST

1 Avenue of
the Palms
Treasure Island
+1 415 898 0245
treasurefest.com

This flea on the island is hosted the last weekend of each month. There are some vintage items to be found, but mostly it's stuff that's been refurbished or made with repurposed materials. It also offers plenty of food trucks and great views of the Bay. There are many wineries to visit there, too.

494 STUFF

150 Valencia Street
Mission ⑤
+1 415 864 2900
stuffsf.com

Inside this massive 1600-square-meter space are two floors full of antiques, vintage pieces and collectibles of all kinds spanning many style periods. Walk through the aisles and peruse all the goods offered by each vendor. Stock is replenished continuously, so grab that coveted piece before it's gone.

495 ALAMEDA POINT ANTIQUES FAIRE

2900 Navy Way
GPS: 3800 Main St
Alameda
+1 510 522 7500
alamedapoint antiquesfaire.com

This is the largest and most popular flea market held the first Sunday of each month from 6 am to 3 pm. Entry fee is scaled based on what time you get there. Early birds get first dibs on the goods. Plan on being here for several hours. It's that big.

5 spots for
A PERFECT PICNIC

---

496 CRISSY FIELD

Presidio ①

*parksconservancy.org/
programs/crissy-field-
center*

A popular spot along the waterfront by the Golden Gate Bridge with large stretches of flat grassy fields and a beach, too. There are picnic tables with barbeque pits, but you need to rise early and get to them before others do. Bring a bike, kite, volleyball and some lawn games.

497 MISSION DOLORES PARK

19th and Dolores St
Mission ⑤

*sfrecpark.org/
destination/mission-
dolores-park*

This large park is located in the sunniest part of town and is very popular given its location to so many amenities (markets, cafes, ice-cream shops) and its spectacular views of the city. Expect plenty of sun worshippers in their skivvies on a hot day. There's a fantastic playground for kids to enjoy, too.

498 SOUTH PARK

64 South Park Ave
South Beach ③
sfrecpark.org/
destination/south-park

For a real hidden gem of a picnic spot, find this very tiny and quiet park surrounded by a circle of homes and businesses. During the weekdays it's mostly inhabited by those working for nearby tech firms, but it's calm and peaceful any day. There's a cool play structure for kids to enjoy.

499 WASHINGTON SQUARE PARK

Union Street and
Columbus Avenue
North Beach/
Telegraph Hill ②

Grab a sandwich at nearby Molinari Deli, then plop down and enjoy it at this park located in the heart of North Beach. Find yourself surrounded by historic churches, old bakeries, cafes and quaint shops. A known spot for daily tai chi and free movie nights during the warm season.

500 SALESFORCE PARK

425 Mission Street
SoMa ③
+1 415 597 5000
salesforcetransit
center.com/
salesforce-park

21 meters above ground is the newest urban garden spanning four city blocks. The park is accessible to all and has walking trails, vast lawns, a children's play area and an amphitheater for free events. Pick up the essentials for a picnic and head up here. Check ahead for operation hours.

APPLE UNION SQUARE – THE PLAZA

INDEX

COLOPHON

EDITING *and* COMPOSING — Leslie Santarina

GRAPHIC DESIGN — Joke Gossé and Sarah Schrauwen

PHOTOGRAPHY — Leslie Santarina — www.spottedsf.com

COVER IMAGE — Helipad House (secret 364)

The addresses in this book have been selected after thorough independent
research by the author, in collaboration with Luster Publishing. The selection
is solely based on personal evaluation of the business by the author. Nothing
in this book was published in exchange for payment or benefits of any kind.

D/2018/12.005/3
ISBN 978 94 6058 2196
NUR 510, 513

© 2018 Luster, Antwerp
Second edition, October 2019 – First reprint, October 2019
www.lusterweb.com – WWW.THE500HIDDENSECRETS.COM
info@lusterweb.com

Printed in Italy by Printer Trento.

All rights reserved.
No part of this publication may be reproduced,
stored in a retrieval system, or transmitted, in
any form or by any means, without the prior
written consent of the publisher. An exception is
made for short excerpts which may be cited for
the sole purpose of reviews.